CONGREGATIONAL HOUSE.

# PROCEEDINGS

AT THE

*DEDICATION*

OF THE

# CONGREGATIONAL HOUSE,

***Boston, February 12th, 1873.***

TOGETHER WITH A

## BRIEF HISTORY

OF THE

## American Congregational Association,

BY THE

CORRESPONDING SECRETARY.

---

BOSTON:
AMERICAN CONGREGATIONAL ASSOCIATION.
1873.

# INTRODUCTION.

The following pages are issued in accordance with a vote of the Directors of the American Congregational Association, at their meeting holden February 20, 1873.

The services herein detailed were conducted in Pilgrim Hall on the fourth floor of the Congregational House. In it and in the adjoining committee room, seats were provided to accommodate six hundred and eleven persons. These were all occupied, and in the doorways and corridors were many standing. The close and patient attention of such a crowded audience for over three hours gave unequivocal testimony to the pertinency and ability of the several performances.

The superadded sketch of the origin and progress of the Association to the present, is intended to give the reader some idea of the work done, and the obstacles encountered in gaining the results already assured.

The Charter, Constitution, and By-Laws, together with a list of the Officers of the Association, will be a convenience to those who may wish to know its basis and present working force.

# ORDER OF EXERCISES.

---

## 1. SINGING.

BY THE CONGREGATION.

*"Coronation."*

All hail the power of Jesus' name !
  Let angels prostrate fall ;
Bring forth the royal diadem,
  And crown him Lord of all.

Ye chosen seed of Israel's race,
  Ye ransomed from the fall,
Hail him who saves you by his grace,
  And crown him Lord of all.

Let every kindred, every tribe,
  On this terrestrial ball
To him all majesty ascribe,
  And crown him Lord of all.

---

## 2. INVOCATION AND READING SCRIPTURES.

By Prof. Hiram Mead, Oberlin, Ohio.

---

## 3. INTRODUCTORY REMARKS.

By Hon. E. S. Tobey, *President American Congregational Association.*

---

## 4. ADDRESS.

By Rev. Wm. Ives Budington, D. D., Brooklyn, N. Y.

## 5. DEDICATORY PRAYER.

BY REV. E. N. KIRK, D. D., BOSTON.

---

## 6. SINGING.

Thy name we bless, Almighty God!
  For all the kindness thou hast shown,
To this fair land the Pilgrims trod, —
  This land we fondly call our own.

We praise thee, that the gospel's light,
  Through all our land its radiance sheds;
Dispels the shades of error's night,
  And heavenly blessings round us spreads.

---

## 7. BRIEF REMARKS.

BY REV. RUFUS ANDERSON, D. D.
DEA. EZRA FARNSWORTH, *Chairman of Building Committee.*
REV. ISAAC P. LANGWORTHY, *Corresponding Secretary.*
REV. H. M. DEXTER, D. D. (Presenting a stone from Scrooby.)
DR. TIMOTHY GORDON, (Presenting a piece of genuine Plymouth Rock.)
GOV. W. B. WASHBURN.
HON. EMORY WASHBURN, Cambridge.
PROF. E. A. PARK, D. D., Andover.

---

## DOXOLOGY.

---

## BENEDICTION.

BY REV. E. B. WEBB, D. D., BOSTON.

# INTRODUCTORY ADDRESS.

BY THE HON. E. S. TOBEY, PRESIDENT.

---

In behalf of the American Congregational Association, it becomes my agreeable duty to congratulate the contributors to the Congregational House, and the denomination which it represents, upon its completion, and I wish it were possible to add, the completion also of the adjoining library building. It gives me pleasure now to welcome you to a participation in the service of dedicating this building to the noble purposes for which it was designed. The idea of establishing this enterprise, when first placed before the churches, appeared too indefinite and abstract to command at once the ready approval and favorable response which its earnest friends desired, and hence the arduous efforts and almost importunate appeals for means to execute the purpose of its original projectors. The long delay in procuring adequate pecuniary aid, and of securing a proper site, has found a parallel in the fact that it required nearly ten years, in the great and wealthy metropolis of England, to carry into effect a similar object. As usual, persevering and unremitting energy, based on a true and worthy idea, has finally prevailed in both instances; and now that this structure, in all its commodious and attractive arrangements, is before us, we may hope that its practical value and usefulness will be no longer doubted. Indeed, I cannot resist the conviction that from this day of its dedication a steadily increasing interest will be evinced.

With a fragment of the "Manor House" in Scrooby, the gift of the Rev. Dr. Dexter, who brought it from England, and with a portion of the veritable Plymouth Rock, presented by Dr. Gordon, now before us, to be deposited in the library of choice and ancient books, this house may be regarded as a sort of "Pilgrim shrine" towards which the descendants of the Pilgrims will instinctively bend their steps whenever they shall visit this city, and for which the voluntary contributors on the shores of the Pacific, in the Sandwich Islands, or in distant India, who may never visit it, will ever entertain a reverential regard, if not a fond attachment, as already expressed in the sentiments which have accompanied their gifts.

A granite monument in Plymouth stands in silent grandeur to commemorate one of the most sublime events in human history. This granite building is also a monument to the principles and church polity of the fathers, not teaching alone by its material form, but instinct with a living influence through the moral power of the societies gathered within its walls.

From the Congregational Home will radiate the influences of the gospel to all nations, through the agencies of the American Board of Commissioners for Foreign Missions, and the Woman's Board of Missions. From here also the American Missionary Association, the Massachusetts Home Missionary Society, the American Congregational Union, the City Missionary Society, the Congregational Publishing Society, the Congregational Quarterly, and the Congregational weekly newspaper, will each in their appropriate sphere, with ever-increasing energy, send forth their beneficent and Christian efforts to elevate the character of the masses of the people of our own country; while the American Peace Society, in co-operation with kindred associations in foreign countries, stimulated by the results of the Geneva arbitration, is even now actively engaged in efforts to bring into existence a code of international laws to provide henceforth for the peaceful solution of disputed questions between nations, and avert the dread calamity of war. Thus will these societies, from this source of moral power, ever be contributing to the perpetuity of the principles of the fathers of the Republic, and of the institutions which they founded.

In the library of this Association, comprising now about fifteen thousand volumes, are rare and valuable works of the able writers and profound theologians of by-gone centuries. These, accessible and especially useful to the student and the historian, will by the perpetual force of truth continue to give direction to opinion, and perhaps exert more or less controlling influence on the minds of men for generations to come.

To preserve these literary treasures it only remains that the interior of the fire-proof library building already erected, and forming a part of this house, shall be speedily finished. While this structure combines all the conveniences which an entirely new one could have furnished, it is obvious that its style of architecture is not only unambitious, but severely plain. This, however, with its massive and enduring material, may perhaps render it the more appropriate symbol of Congregationalism. In this progressive age it may ultimately yield to the advancing wave of commerce, but all that is vital in the institution itself will endure, even when transferred to some more favored locality and to a building commensurate with the new and greater demands of the future. But for many years hence, no location could combine greater advantages, dependent in part, as it now is, on a commercial foundation and surroundings for revenue.

It has been alleged that the tendency of Congregationalism is to promote an undue sense of personal independence and individualism at the expense of mutual sympathy and even of social qualities. If this is in any degree true, let us hope that this institution may to some extent serve to promote more intimate personal relations, and strengthen the bonds of sympathy and of friendship between brethren of the same Christian faith, as they shall statedly gather in this hall for social intercourse, as well as for the discussion of religious topics of mutual interest. May we not properly cultivate a deeper interest in, and a laudable partiality for, the denomination with which we are connected, while at the same time we are careful to cherish a catholic spirit towards those of a different faith, always esteeming a comprehensive spirit of genuine Christianity as superior to all denominational or sectarian preferences.

Every intelligent Congregationalist should be able to exercise a discriminating judgment as to the character of our peculiar church polity, and become so familiar with its relations to the foundation of civil government and republican institutions in our country as to know on how firm and true a basis his opinions rest. Within the last few years a new impulse has been given to the public mind on this subject, and information has been more widely diffused through the pulpit and the press.

If in connection with the frequent appeals and arguments put forth in advocacy of the usefulness of the institution which we are now about to dedicate, anything has been done to promote a more thorough examination and better understanding of Congregationalism, one at least of its practical objects will have been already attained.

But the proprieties of the occasion forbid that I should enlarge on these topics, and I therefore at once give place to the distinguished gentlemen who are to follow in these exercises.

# ADDRESS.

BY REV. WM. IVES BUDINGTON, D.D.

---

MR. PRESIDENT, LADIES, AND GENTLEMEN:

I rise with pleasure to respond to the invitation with which I am honored, to address you, and join my felicitations with yours on the consummation of this significant enterprise. While it would be more grateful to my feelings to sit at the feet of some whom I see around me, I am willing to take the place your courtesy has assigned me, because I feel that I am representing before you the sons of New England, *out of* New England; and venturing for a moment to speak for them, I bring you the heart-felt congratulations of the children of the Pilgrims scattered over this broad land, from the Hudson to the Pacific.

You have done well to build a house for God, — I say *for God*, for the Temple at Jerusalem was not more truly built for the offering of sacrifice to Jehovah than is this. The difference is only the difference between the Mosaic and the Christian dispensations. From every part of the land, from altars of Christian households and Christian churches, all over the continent, are to come hither the sacrifices of our people to send the gospel round the world, and make all the families of the earth akin, by making them believers in the common name of Christ. I thank you for building such a house to receive such sacrifices; and I speak not now of contributions of money, but contributions of our sons and daughters. What memories throng in our minds, at an hour like this, of the sacrifices that have been laid on the altar of God, in yonder house on Pemberton Square! What goodly companies have gone from the rooms of the Home Missionary Society! And may God spare this building for generations to come, till all its rooms shall be consecrated by larger and better sacrifices to Him, who gave himself, once for all, for us and for the whole world! Such a house is worthy to be builded by all our churches, and worthy to be called the house of God, as glorious as that which stood on Mount Moriah and more so, — as much more so as the living sacrifices to be offered here exceed the typical ones that bled there.

You have put the word "Congregational" upon this house. Am I not right in saying, that this is the first time in our history, that this, our distinctive name, has been placed upon a structure erected by the general contributions of our churches? The earliest denomination of Christians to occupy this western world, has thus been the last to assert itself denominationally. In the winter of 1620–1, the Pilgrims found for themselves a permanent home in Plymouth; in the winter of 1872–3, their principles of church-order first find a lodgment in the city they founded and have made illustrious.

What is the meaning of this? Does it signify a change on the part of our churches and people? Are we more sectarian than our fathers were? Are we attaching to our polity an importance which its framers did not, but which for two centuries and a half has been substantially ignored, and left to care for itself?

It is a question pertinent to the hour, and one to which our people are peculiarly sensitive. Let me answer it; but before doing so, let me say, what will not be denied, and cannot be, that our people have from the first been eminently catholic. The Pilgrims were so in Holland. Edward Winslow testifies, from personal knowledge as a parishioner, to the broad and sweet charity of John Robinson, which in that age was wonderful, and in this is still beautiful. He repudiates for his teacher the name and spirit of "Separatist," and recites the communion he practised with the Dutch and French churches, as well as with the churches of England and Scotland. And in this country, when our churches were originally gathered, the name "Congregational" was not used as a designation; it was, you remember, the "First Church, Plymouth," "First Church, Boston," or Hartford, or New Haven. It seems a tautology, as the words "congregation" and "church" had the same meaning, and represented the same original word. During the greater part of our history since, not Christian polity, but Christian doctrine, has been thought of, discussed, and prized; and consequently our people have known no difference, not even in name, between themselves and our Presbyterian brethren, who have espoused the same views of divine truth. Accordingly, when our people moved west, they easily coalesced with other bodies of Christians, especially the Presbyterians, and were not conscious of making a change. Dr. Nott, the late President of Union College, told me that he considered himself largely responsible for this course of things in the State of New York; thinking it a pity, he said, that there should be two denominations in place of one; and coming from Connecticut, as he did, he proposed to his brother on the ground, representing Presbyterianism, that they should organize churches after one pattern, and bearing a common name.

This tendency has been expressed, and still further increased, by the formation of union societies for the propagation of the gospel. It was natural, under their circumstances unavoidable, that our fathers, when they came to organize missionary societies, should do it irrespective of church polity; in their view, the gospel was the light from heaven, and church polity no more than the window that let the light through. The less it was thought of, the less it detained of the light to reveal its own existence, the better. Thus foreign missions and home missions were first organized by Congregationalists, but irrespective of name, and in concert with Christians of like faith. But I need not tell you, that now, with no thought of ours, and by no action on our part, this co-operative union has been broken up. The providence of God has evidently been concerned in the movement, and we have nothing to do but to bow to it. Church action has been substituted in place of union and voluntary associations. The result is, that we find ourselves substantially in possession of the great organizations, which remain unchanged upon their catholic basis, but which look for support mainly to Congregational churches, — I mean the American Home Missionary Society and the A. B. C. F. M.

What, now, are we to do? Forced back upon ourselves, we have been obliged to ask the question, What *are* the principles of church order by which we are distinguished, and have they claims upon our advocacy and support? We must either abandon our polity, confess that Congregationalism has no permanent mission in the land, and so merge ourselves in other denominations; or we must adhere to the principles we have received from our fathers, honor them, and sustain them. The Society of Friends have been giving signs — at least, many of them — that they have accomplished their distinctive mission: having borne a long and honorable testimony to the power and preciousness of the indwelling Spirit of God, they find this truth heartily welcomed by other Christians, and admitting for themselves the sanctity of sacramental forms, they are seeking new homes in other communions. Is it to be so with us? No doubt our Congregational principles have found their way, along with our people, into churches that were formerly hostile to them, but which have been gradually leavened by them. The unit with us, according to our polity, is the local church; as in Presbyterianism it is the presbytery, and in Episcopacy the diocese. Now, in point of fact, it will be found that the autonomy of the local church has gone beyond the recognition of the principle. In the supreme judicatories of national churches, authority is less and less appealed to, and government more and more exercised in a declarative and advisory way. Perhaps the most thoroughly organized and manifoldly self-active church in the city of New York is the "Holy Trinity," under the pastoral care of the younger Dr. Tyng. It is Episcopal in name, but Congregational in spirit. Its distinctive history has been made by its development of the local church or parish. It reproduces, in many features, the early Congregation, presided over by a board of Presbyters, in which the bishop was first among his equals. With Dr. Tyng as rector are associated not less than seven ministers, who have in charge as many chapels, surrounding the mother church; to these are added mission schools, lay missionaries, a dispensary, infirmary, orphanage, a girls' sewing school, Dorcas societies, and a House of Evangelists, which is a training school for Christian workers.

Now, is our mission ended? Shall we content ourselves with an influence unconsciously exerted and unconsciously felt? I ask this question and answer it, alone in the spirit of loyalty to the great Head of the Church, and of zeal for the unity of his body on earth. I speak for myself, and I am sure I speak for the builders of this house, when I say that we value our polity only as it subserves the kingdom of Christ; we are Congregationalists because we are Christians, and because under the forms of our polity, we think we can best compass the evangelization of the world, and best bring together the churches of Christ in oneness of body and spirit. If our polity be a schism, or tend to a schism, we will have nothing to do with it; it is only in the interest of true religion and of catholicity that we espouse it, and will maintain it.

What is the Congregational polity? In substance, the autonomy of the local church, — the complete church estate of every body of associated believers, as having Christ in the midst of them, and being by him made the recipient of the faith, and the depository of church rule. To this is only to be added the free and unconstrained fellowship of the churches, — a fellowship springing from the churches themselves, and not imposed by bodies outside of, and independent of, the local church.

Look at this theory of the church, as to its place in history. We hold it to be the earliest organization. "We," do I say? Am I not warranted in saying, it is now conceded matter of fact, and admitted by many who nevertheless regard later constitutions as legitimate and better? The Christian scholarship of this nineteenth century has settled some things. It is impossible to go over, in the manner of our fathers, some of the great questions that have hitherto divided the churches of the Reformation. The dissertation of Dr. Lightfoot, of the University of Cambridge in England, on "The Christian Ministry," by its candor and large-minded intelligence, must banish certain phases of the Episcopal controversy. We freely own that the Congregational way of church government was too free and spiritual for the first centuries of the Christian era, that it demanded too much intelligence and self-control for Christianity in its first stages. So Judaism with its monotheism was too spiritual for the Israelites in the desert, and long after they were settled on the hills of Palestine, overshadowed as they were by the idolatries of the great kingdoms about them. But it is God's way to give truth to educate peoples, and He teaches that it is better to make it known, even though it be corrupted and overlaid for long periods, and that it will fight its way back, and suffer its way back, and in the end be all the clearer and the stronger for the discipline. So it has proved with the Congregational polity. Within three or four hundred years it has reappeared, and come as the most advanced thought, the ripest fruit of the Reformation in England. There is something significant in the method and time of this reappearance. Like Wesleyanism, it had its origin in an English university; but unlike it, not bearing its paternity in its name, it grew up simultaneously in a multitude of minds, not alone in sequestered study, but in busy pastorships, not alone among the clergy, but the people as well. It was the final outcome of the reformed Church of England, her martyrs, confessors, and heroes. If anything in the history of the Christian church ever had its roots in strong thinking and earnest living, it was that historical movement which gave England her liberty and America her constitution. What honor did God put upon the Pilgrims of Holland and the Puritans of England, and the polity they revived, to make *them* and *it* the bond of union between the old world and the new, — final fruits of the history consummated there, and seed-principles of the history inaugurated here!

We are not instituting extravagant and distasteful claims for Congregational churches, as the *best* churches, much less as the *only* churches of Christ in our time. We are only asserting that to them are committed principles more sacred than they know, the nature of which they only partly comprehend, in the development of which they are feeble and hesitating, but the value of which is becoming more and more apparent as the needs and dangers of our time become more conspicuous. Viewed not as a *sect-principle*, but a *law of development* deduced from the Scriptures, and illustrated by primitive practice, the church polity, which makes the congregation the fountain of power and the unit of aggregation, belongs not to the form but to the life of Christianity,— it is a doctrine as well as a government.

The great apostasy of Romanism is but an illustration of the importance attaching to the polity of the church; and it is the development of the world-idea of power and authority, which began so early to supplant the simple and self-active fellowships of the Apostles' days; and as in point of fact it has been the occasion of reviving the primitive polity, so it is most directly met and antagonized by this polity. The grace of salvation, according to the Romish theory, is a deposit intrusted to a few men, in effect to *one* man, who infallibly declares the will of God, and infallibly imparts the grace of God, to such as recognize his authority, and seek salvation as he directs. By that theory the body of the church are made to receive spiritual life from the officers of the church, and so are absolutely dependent upon them. The Congregational theory is precisely the reverse of all this. The body of the church receives directly from God, through faith in Christ, a divine life, which is the inspiration of the Holy Spirit; and in that life is given ministry, sacrament, self-government, and world-wide diffusion. "Where two or three are gathered together in my name, there am I in the midst of them." Hence all the sacredness and power of the church. The sublimest institution on earth is a church recognizing the presence of Christ in the midst of them, and obeying his Spirit. There can be no more valid ministry than that which such a church elects, and sets apart by prayer and imposition of hands. There are no more valid sacraments than those which such believers observe in the faith of their present Lord. The validity of church organization, of ministry and sacrament, the "power of the keys," so called, does not come from the past, by succession of inheritance and bequest; does not come from *without*, but from *within*, from the ever-present spirit of life in the hearts of believers. God is its author and inspirer to-day, as when the first church came together in Jerusalem. The church springs, as government does, from the hearts of the people; from within outwards, from beneath upwards, is the course of spiritual life and growth.

See how marked the contrast, how exact the contradiction between the Romish and the Congregational theory. The Romanist says the life and life-imparting grace of salvation resides in the Holy Father, and only by communion with Him, is preserved to bishops, priests, and people. The Congregationalist says that the grace of salvation is given to the congregation of Christ's faithful people, through whom from Christ, by his express appointment, come pastors and teachers, and without whom is neither church ordinance nor act. The Congregationalist, also, in his way is as much a *churchman* as the Romanist in his. *Churchman* is only another word for *Congregationalist*, inasmuch as congregation and church are the same thing. Is the church to the Romanist a divine institution? So and not less is it to us. Has the Roman Catholic polity to do with the essence of Christianity itself? So and not less has the Congregational, which is the reaffirmation of our Lord's own teaching, that Christ, in the midst, is the being and the life of the church, his life permeating theirs, and thus making the church to become the body of Christ. So we meet the Romanist on his own ground. He can take no higher position than we do. It is doctrine meeting doctrine. This fits us pre-eminently to confront the power of Rome. On this new continent, and beneath new conditions, the church of Rome is to contend with primitive Christianity clothed with her primitive polity. The impending conflict we believe to be the last; but it will be the *first* in which Romanism and Congregationalism have met upon a fair field. For this reason, therefore, because our polity gives us the vantage-ground in the great controversy with Rome, we are bound to affirm it, by the highest consideration that can take hold of us, either as Christians or as citizens.

But there is another reason that binds us to this. We are upon the eve of great doctrinal agitations. We have Romanism on one side, and a godless infidelity on the other; and our Congregationalism will be found to be as necessary in combating the one as the other. The church of God has had heresies to contend with before, but the most damnable of all is approaching. The coming question is not, Whether Christ be the supreme head of the church, and entitled to our absolute allegiance as King and Lord, but it is a question deeper than this, Whether there *be any King or Lord in the universe?* A class of doubters has sprung into notice, who tell us that if God is not in creation, he does not exist at all so far as men are concerned, for the Universe alone is knowable; and if there be a God somewhere else, he is not a being who has any rights we are bound to respect. In confronting this last and boldest assault upon the faith once delivered to the saints, it is most important that Christians be united and firm in the testimony they bear to the truth of God. It is indispensable that petty and divisive questions be driven from the church of God, and that an unbroken front be presented to the atheism and irreligion of our times. We must have a polity that is comprehensive of all faithful men; and that polity alone will meet the exigencies of the present and the coming age, which allows for and combines all the diversities of belief necessitated by nature and tolerated by the Spirit of God.

The great problem has been, and still is, how to make the church comprehensive, and at the same time faithful to the deposit of the faith. The true catholic church, it has been universally conceded, must be tolerant of differences having their origin in God's ordinations, in race and nationality, in temperament and culture, in civilization and refinement. But practically the problem has been found insoluble, where to run the line between those essential doctrines which cannot be denied without denying the faith, and those other doctrines, which, though belonging to it, may be separated from it, to the *harm* indeed, but not to the *destruction* of the whole. What has seemed essential to one has not seemed so to another; what is so regarded in one age, is not so looked upon in another. Two methods have been resorted to. Confessions, in the first instance, have been drawn up, declaring what the framers thought to be true, and assent to them has been required on pain of eternal damnation. The enlightened, and I will add the Christian, sentiment of the world is becoming more and more settled in opposition to such tests of Christian character, and such conditions of salvation. Of this the present agitation is witness, in the Church of England, against the damnatory clauses of the so-called Athanasian creed; and the beginning discussions, as well, respecting the Westminster Confession in the Church of Scotland. The other way has been to select general statements, and adopt venerable, historic symbols for substance of doctrine. But the more generic these statements have been made, the weaker they have become as bonds of union, and the more diverse the parties they have included, till they have ceased to perform the functions of a common confession. So that it has come to pass, that these attempts to express the ancient faith in modern moulds of thoughts, whether in strict or liberal articles of agreement, have been patent failures, and are well-nigh acknowledged to be such. The problem seems beyond human solution; and we have no reason to regret it, for it is not in this way that the unity of Christ's church is to be expressed and maintained.

The Congregational way has been to deny the right

or utility of such confessions; to insist that they have no binding force upon the local church; and to remand the confession of the faith once delivered to the saints to each assemblage of believers, to whom it originally belonged, and whence it has been mischievously taken. It has been to refer the confession of the truths of the gospel to men and women in the midst of actual life, and remote from all metaphysical speculations, and thus bring to the front the concrete facts of the incarnation, the death, and resurrection of our Lord, and the outpouring of the Holy Spirit, the Lord and giver of life. It is to rest the security and perpetuation of the faith on the testimony of living disciples, whose lives and experiences are facts that hold in them the divine deposit. It is, in other words, to repose confidence in the Spirit of God, present and ruling in the hearts of God's people. It is to go back to the sublime example of Christ and his Apostles; of Christ, who wrote not a line, but contented himself with pouring his life into the hearts of men; of the Apostles, who made themselves witnesses to the facts of a divine life, and their converts to be epistles, "written not with ink, but with the Spirit of the living God."

The church has been slow to learn the possibility and safety of doing this. But what has been the consequence of leaving the utterance and defence of the gospel to the separate congregations of believers? We appeal to actual results, to an unanimity of believing and fellowshipping, never attained under subscription to national or ecumenical creeds. Mere results are sufficient, we hold, to establish the principle. It is safe, safest of all, to entrust the keeping of the faith to churches made up of plain people, believing in their hearts, and confessing with their mouths, what they have received and known and felt of the great salvation. The Independent and Baptist churches of Great Britain, as well as of this country, have maintained the fundamental doctrines of the gospel more harmoniously than any like number of believers, for a like period of time, since the Christian era.

This action of our churches, however, has been taken with no prejudice to the rightful province of theology. It only remands it, where it belongs, to the schools, and to the doctors of the church. In its sphere theology is as useful, and as necessary, as science is in its sphere. But as bread existed before chemistry was born, and will be made and eaten as before by multitudes ignorant of its chemical equivalents, so the faith of Christ, the manna of the soul, antedated theology, and will continue to be preached and received, in all its saving power, by many who are ignorant of the elements of theological science. The gospel was originally delivered to men in the concrete, and chiefly in the life of one incomparable Being; and this gospel, in its original shape, is sufficient for pulpit, communion-table, prayer-meeting, and closet. In this way, and for this reason, the unity of our churches has been maintained, as it never could have been, in the midst of contending theologies, had any one of them had the right, or been permitted to impose itself upon the churches. The communion of Congregational churches cannot be permanently interrupted, till the great facts of the gospel history are denied, and the practical manifestations of the Christian life are given up. You might as well draw dividing lines through the fluent waters, as between free and independent churches, living a common life, and practically holding the same faith in Christ. We hold it, therefore, as demonstrated by experience, that the Congregational polity admits of the widest possible comprehension, and this without laxity of doctrine, or the surrender of the faith.

So, too, Congregationalism is comprehensive in respect to modes of worship; for these, along with confessions of faith, are left with the local church. And this is a blessed feature in our polity, especially as we look into the future. In the first instance, no doubt, preaching is so important as to be the almost exclusive concern of ministers and churches. The gospel must be known before the God of the gospel can become the object of worship. Preaching is the great work of the missionary, carrying the gospel to the heathen; and of the evangelist, as well, in great cities and neglected neighborhoods. But when men are converted, and settled in well-ordered families and congregations, worship becomes much more an object of interest and concern to minister and people, till, in the advancement of intellectual and spiritual culture, it becomes the great end, and preaching introductory and subservient to it. The prominence that of late has been given to prayer-meetings, and the power they have had in awakening and diffusing religious interest, is remarkable, and suggestive of the tendency of the public mind. There is a power in worship we have only begun to realize; and in many of our congregations there is an unmistakable demand for more *common* worship, — for modes which will enable all to take part. It is a want coming from the deepest consciousness of the Christian life. Worship never tires, always interests and feeds; that is, true worship does. Worship is life itself, while instruction, however necessary, is only preparatory to life. The desire for it, also, marks a higher stage of Christian character and growth. There comes a time when the intelligent, well-furnished mind is settled and fixed in the knowledge of fundamental doctrines, when a reconsideration of them, in the way of argument and defence, has a weakening, rather than strengthening effect, and to such an one worship becomes a hunger and a necessity. Now the polity which intrusts to the local church the duty of self-government, is a means of growth and development in this most important matter of ordering the worship of God. It says to the people, do it in the way your own thoughtful and prayerful study of the subject shall convince you will be most for your spiritual good, and your children's. No authority from without imposes one and the same mode upon all congregations, irrespective of taste, training, or culture; but they are called upon to apply their intelligence and experience to the question, and whatever modes have approved themselves on trial, whether among themselves or other Christians, whether in this age or other ages, they are at perfect liberty to adopt and practice. In this way, worship, like creed-making, which has been a divisive subject, is no longer a source of schism, but, belonging to the recognized rights and duties of each separate congregation, becomes a means of educating the people, and making their worship a manifestation of the church's life.

In this way, with no departure from principle, our communion may be diversified by all the manifold varieties which the hand and Spirit of God create, and it thus becomes possible for all true and earnest Christians to find a congenial home among us. We have nothing to fear from the manifoldness of method, which earnest thought and freedom will generate; on the contrary, our greatest danger is, that the Congregational polity will not be put to the proof by being used, that the *right* of the people will not also be regarded as a *duty*. We have left things to drift, rather than to be governed by the enlightened minds and Spirit-led consciences of our people, applying themselves, under a sense of responsibility, to the study of their concerns, and acting in the exercise of their best judgment. If Congregational churches do not use their freedom, but allow themselves to be controlled by self-constituted judges, and kept stationary by the dead-weight of tradition, they lose all the advantages of their distinctive polity, while of course they fail of those which are distinctive of centralized and consolidated church governments. Our fathers said they came hither to practise the *positive* part of church reformation. In England they were necessarily confined to the *negative* part: they were *protesters*, *deniers*. The First Church, Boston, was full of this formative, originating life,—"the most glorious church in the world," an early New-England historian said he really believed it was; and for this very reason, that they put into practice whatever commended itself to them as being wise and good. What John Cotton propounded to them out of the Word of God, they discussed; and if they could say, "It seems good to the Holy Ghost and to us," they proceeded to put it into legislation, or set it up as an institution. This is the life of our polity; it is capable of indefinite expansion, and the hope of our churches and of the world is in it.

We must entertain a higher sense of the supernatural power and sacredness of the local church, as dwelt in by the church's Lord. It is the most sacred thing on earth, next to the human soul. The church is of more importance than the ministry, for it is the author of it. The minister is never more truly Christ's servant, than when he develops the individual life of the individual church. Genius and learning are, no doubt, precious gifts, and so precious that the church will be in no danger of undervaluing them. But when the minister overshadows the church, and the people gather around him, as the informing genius of the institution, so that when he is present they are, and when he is not, they are not, the distinctive marks of a church are absent; it is an institution, but a human one; the sermons are orations, and the life of the church is that of the lecture-room, the senate, or the academy.

I will detain you to speak of but one more reason why we should avow and defend the polity of the Congregational churches. It is our best, I think I must say, our *only* hope of the unity of Christ's universal church. By eliminating legislative and judicial functions from the representative assemblies of our churches, it takes away from us the great causes of schism in all ages, and brings in themes of universal concern and sympathy. It spends the force of our united churches upon forms of power and manifestations of life, which are the highest and best. By the fundamental law of our system, the deliverances made in general council depend for their influence upon the reason that is in them. Two benefits flow from this. The first is to the council itself, that it be moved to do nothing, which heart and mind alike are not convinced of, and *so* convinced of, as to be persuaded of the Holy Spirit's guidance. The other is that such deliverances, when thus made, are more powerful over Christian churches than any other can be. Their effect is to be measured only by the intelligence and conscience of the people, which are aroused by them, and made to execute them. In other words, this form of church government executes itself, and perhaps never more completely than when it rouses opposition; it is bounded only by the limits of Christianity itself. Beyond this it cannot go, and beyond this no church power can go, without injury to Christian character and growth. No combinations of Congregational churches can be made for sectarian aggrandizement. They live only in consenting judgments, and act only through harmonious spirits.

But while they are powerless for evil, they are efficient for good. They lay the foundation for co-operation among all Christians. On the basis of the divinely ordered independence of the local church, including, as a matter of course, the right of each body of believers to form such affiliations as it chooses, there is a platform of union broad enough for all communions.

This has been beautifully illustrated of late in New York. The council called to install Mr. Hepworth over the "Church of the Disciples," gathered by himself, exhibited what the polity is capable of, which conserves the autonomy of the local church, and asks recognition from neighboring and differing communions. The examination, and solemn setting apart to the Christian ministry, of a man asking it in the name of Christ, is one of the most distinctive acts of church rule. Denominations that can unite in this, can unite in all that is necessary to express and preserve the unity of the church, — *the unity of the Spirit in the bond of peace.* But that council, summoned to do that work and doing it, was made up of representatives from churches differing from one another in many and confessedly important subjects of doctrine and polity. Besides Congregationalists, there were Baptist, Episcopal, Methodist, and Presbyterian delegates. We have no disposition to claim it as a Congregational body, in any sectarian and divisive sense; we repudiate the claim, and the spirit that makes it. We only insist upon it, that there is a common and recognized polity among us, upon which all churches of Christ can meet and act together, without dishonor to their distinctive views, with no advantage of one over the other, and yet in the manifestation of a real and substantial unity, finding a real and substantial expression. In this respect the "Church ot the Disciples" did what the older and honored "Tabernacle Church" did not do, when calling, as they recently did, a council to install a pastor, coming to them from the Presbyterian communion, they invited delegates from that and other Christian bodies, as guests, and not as constituent members of the council without a distinction between them and delegates from Congregational churches. The "Church of the Disciples," in doing as they have done, have demonstrated a practicable way of communion between different Christian organizations, and one sufficient for practical purposes, and capable of application to all Evangelical bodies. Occasion has also been given for the manifestation of a most catholic spirit, not less on the part of those accepting, than on the part of the church inviting. The "Church of the Holy Trinity" was recognized, as we all recognize it, as a true church of Christ, and that church recognized the "Church of the Disciples" in the exercise of its right, as on the one hand to unite with the diocese and submit to Episcopal supervision, so on the other to associate itself with other bodies of Christian believers, *not* united to the diocese, and not subject to Episcopal oversight. The rector of that church, in an admirable and most Evangelical charge, committed the care of souls in the newly gathered congregation to Mr. Hepworth. It was a proclamation to the Christians of New York, that the Episcopal ordering and classification of churches might remain, and still permit of a real and most solemn union with non-Episcopal churches. It was the reinauguration of the fellowship which subsisted between the Reformed Church of England, and the Reformed Churches of the Continent, in the days of England's martyr bishops and confessors.

We are also about to witness in our country an *Ecumenical Protestant Council*, representing all Evangelical churches throughout Christendom, and meeting together on the basis of their mutual independence, and no less of fellowship and co-operation, arising from the actual union existing between true believers. They meet to discuss principles and announce their consenting judgments respecting the world-wide interests of the church of Christ, and these deliverances of theirs will have as much power as they ought to have, that is all that belongs to the reason that is in them, and the mind of Christ they evince. Meeting on such a basis as this, it were absurd for one class of Christians to claim that another had surrendered any distinctive principle; and yet it is made equally evident, that on the basis of mutual independence and consent, there is an actually existing platform, upon which the actually existing unity and coaction of Christians can be expressed.

In the name, then, of our one Lord, and of the one church he has founded, let us hold on to the primitive polity, practised in the Apostles' days, and revived by the fathers of New England. It affords, we believe, a hope of the reunion of Christendom; if it does not, we wait for our brethren to find another and a better. Romanism has one theory of the unity of the church; Congregationalism another: the world is divided between them, and we calmly await the issue.

Let us rise now, and dedicate this building to God. I see before me the venerable man who has been designated to lead us in this act. Let us rise when he rises, and give the house to God, meaning what this imports, that we give ourselves to God. As Abraham Lincoln, standing on the ever-memorable battle-field of Gettysburg, consecrated that spot forever in the hearts of his countrymen, by giving himself and those who stood with him to the country's defence; so let us dedicate this building, by here giving ourselves to the God whom our fathers served in their day, and by consecrating our children in all coming generations to serve Him in their time.

# PRAYER.

BY REV. EDWARD N. KIRK, D. D.

---

God of Abraham, God of Israel, God and Father of our Lord Jesus Christ; our pilgrim fathers, obedient to thy call, to glorify thy name, and for Zion's sake, forsook houses and lands, home and country. Trusting thy promises, they toiled and suffered; and we, their descendants, are living this day to recognize in their history and in the results of their sacrifices, toils, and prayers, thy faithfulness. Oh God! thou art faithful; thy faithfulness reacheth unto the clouds. These men relied upon thee. They hoped against hope, and we live to witness their hopes not only realized, but far exceeded. Thanks be to God for the history of the Pilgrims. We thank thee, Oh God! that thou didst vouchsafe to them the grace and light that placed them in advance of sages and philosophers, statesmen and churchmen. Thou, through thy commandments, didst make them wiser than their enemies; they had more understanding than all their teachers, for thy testimonies were their meditation; they understood more than the ancients, for they kept thy precepts. We thank thee that the seed transported in the Mayflower has been transformed into the glorious harvest now brightening the hills and valleys of a continent. These men we recognize as thine instrument to construct the Republic. We thank thee for the Republic, and all the principles incorporated into its institutions. To thy goodness we devoutly trace the fact that on this soil no tyrant, civil or ecclesiastical, dictates to our conscience; that here the Church and the State show the world how to respect each other's rights, and to live in perfect harmony. We thank thee that from Christ our fathers learned that the individual was not made for the institutions, but the institutions for the individual man; that the end of government is to secure the welfare of the governed, and not of the governing class; that the local church has but one master, the Saviour, who died for her; that her glory is found not in her hierarchy, not in her rites, but in the presence and power of thine indwelling Spirit. We thank thee that the Republic stands, while the thrones of despotism are tottering. We thank thee, Oh God, that we are Congregational Republicans.

Father of mercies, God of providence, God of all grace, bless the Republic. Make us worthy of such an ancestry, such a history, and of such an inheritance. Vouchsafe to us to avoid all extremes, to combine a truly catholic spirit with loyalty to our own convictions, to contend earnestly for the faith once delivered to the saints, and live in charity with the enemies of thy word; to welcome every new ray of light from thy word, and humbly to follow only the teachings of thy Spirit.

We are assembled, our God and Saviour, to dedicate this edifice, erected in the metropolis of Pilgrim-land, to thy service, to the glory of the triune Jehovah, Father, Son, and Holy Ghost, to the incarnate Word, the Lamb of God, now on the central throne of Heaven.

Under the solemn sense of our responsibility, and in dependence on thy grace, we promise to employ this structure for no selfish, no party purpose, but for the advancement of thy kingdom and glory. Accept the gift, and make this home of our hearts, this centre of our interests, a fountain of light to the perishing world.

Bless in thine infinite mercy the branch of thy church we represent; the members of this body scattered through the world; the laborers at home and abroad, and the institutions here concentrated.

Our want, Father, is spiritual life in greatly advanced degrees; more of the spirit of our blessed Lord; the love, the self-sacrificing love, that brought Him to clothe his Deity with our humanity.

Accept this expression of our thankfulness, and grant these requests, for Jesus' sake. Amen.

## DEA. EZRA FARNSWORTH

WAS introduced as Chairman of the Building Committee, and as one who had taken a deep interest in this enterprise for years; and though at the head of a firm doing a large business, had given freely of his time and money for its accomplishment.

After alluding to the unfriendly criticisms that had been made upon our adding wooden fronts to these granite buildings, he said the committee were not unaware of the incongruity: but necessity knows no law; we *must* have the income.

When we began our alterations and repairs, we expected that with the funds and subscriptions we had in hand, and what we expected to receive from the Fair, and other sources, we should have completed our plans, which included the exterior of the Library Building, and taken possession of our house free from debt above the mortgages. But circumstances beyond our control reduced our receipts from the Fair, and the fire reduced our receipts and added to our expenses in various ways, so that we find ourselves somewhat in debt. Our rentals will be $25,000 — upwards — which will pay our annual interest, our current expenses, and leave, probably, five to seven thousand dollars yearly for a sinking fund, when once our floating debt is paid.

This is a day of rejoicing; we do not solicit to-day, we only give information. Our work has been done under the direction of Cummings & Sears, architects. Whittlesey & Coffin have done the stone and brick work, Mr. Wm. Hunt the carpentry, Messrs. Smith the iron work, Mr. Perry the painting, and Mr. Walker the steam heating; and, on the whole, it has been done to the satisfaction of the committee, and, we trust, to the satisfaction of our friends present.

One of the largest contracts, and some of the others, have been already settled within the sums agreed upon.

The Congregational House is no longer a myth, a prophecy, but an actual, substantial reality.

Our benevolent societies will nearly all be gathered within its walls, and most of them without increase of expense. The American Board will pay less rent for the thirteen rooms they will occupy here, than they will receive for the house they leave, and these rents will be reduced as our sinking fund increases.

The most powerful, puissant forces of nature are silent. Who can tell how much yonder shaft on Bunker Hill has done to stimulate and perpetuate love of country? Who can estimate what Congregationalism has done, and may do, yes, *must* do in the future of our land.

This is an epoch in our history. We have now a *home.* We will put upon these massive, granite walls, in letters of bronze or iron, Congregational House, so that our children, and our children's children, and every passer-by, may see the name. As every addition of strength and vital force at the heart reports itself at the extremities, so what we do here to-day will be felt by every Congregational church from Maine to Texas, and from Boston to the Pacific coast. Yes, and by every church gathered in heathen lands by the American Board the world over, and by every missionary. There is a vast amount of latent power in our Congregational churches that has never been made available. The social element has not been utilized; but now that we have a home for the Congregational Club, we hope to make it available. The first stone house ever built in Boston was built on this very spot 210 years ago, by Rev. James Allen, and occupied by him and his family for about 150 years, when this house was begun. It is fitting that our Congregational House should stand on this historic spot. My experience and observation have convinced me that to ensure success at the present time, the man of business, and the benevolent society as well, must keep abreast of the times in location and appointments. When our fire-proof library building is completed our work will be done, and we shall look upon 1873 as a year long to be remembered with pleasure by our denomination.

---

## REV. RUFUS ANDERSON, D.D.,

WAS to have made "brief remarks," but was kept away by sickness. These, which he has been requested to write out, would have been substantially as follows:—

It was my privilege to be among the first to embark in this enterprise, and my name appears among the original corporators. The Congregational *Library* was at first the leading idea of Dr. Joseph S. Clark, the Secretary, and hence the Association was popularly known, for a time, as the Congregational *Library* Association; but with me, while I did not undervalue the Library, the grand idea was a Congregational HOUSE, as a central point and hive of the denomination. Unity of feeling, purpose, and aim was what we needed as a denomination, and I believed Boston to be the place, and the only place, for the Congregational House.

As one of the directors, I went to the extent of my ability, in co-operation with my brethren, for securing this all-important result, until I was happy to see, at a recent period, that the thing was secure.

But you will allow me to say, that, in all my public life, I have never been so painfully conscious of discouragements; and it sometimes seemed as if there was no body of Christians in our country, in which the *denominational* feeling was so weak, as in our own Congregational body. I mean something very unlike the *sectarian* feeling; something higher, nobler, rejoicing in the prosperity of every section of Christ's kingdom, but intent on doing its own appropriate work. What we specially needed was some acknowledged sign of unity among us, some recognized central point, which should become a common resort, where we should feel at home, and could meet together without ceremony and form, in our own home as Congregational brethren.

That which I earnestly desired to see before I died, we now behold, — all except the *Library!* The spacious building we now dedicate to the service of God stands grandly in the centre of the city, in the religious centre of our denomination, and, for aught I know, in the centre of the universe; and our societies will shortly be at home here, working under one roof, in one spirit, and to the same great end. Would that the *Library* building were also completed; and then we could lay the top-stone with shoutings of grace, grace! But the walls of the fire-proof Library are already up, and we have an invaluable collection of denominational and missionary literature ready to go into it, and the great enterprise will soon be completed. We have begun to build as a denomination, in the name of the King of Zion, and He will enable us to finish.

---

## REV. ISAAC P. LANGWORTHY,

Corresponding Secretary and Financial Agent of the Association, on being introduced, spoke substantially as follows: —

MR. PRESIDENT, AND FRIENDS:

I rejoice in being able to congratulate the directors of the American Congregational Association, on so far completing a work which has borne so heavily for so long a time upon their shoulders. From the Chairman of the Building Committee you have just heard; but of his patient and self-sacrificing labors in this behalf, it is but just that I should on this occasion bear unequivocal testimony. The President of the Association, from whom you have also heard, and who is also a member of that committee, has been from the beginning a ready and willing helper in the same direction. Another of the five, J. P. Melledge, Esq., and from whom you will not hear, was for fifteen years the Treasurer of this Association, and thus understood both its needs and resources. He has freely given the timely aid his peculiar advantages have qualified him to impart. Another, H. D. Hyde, Esq., from whose zeal and counsel much could well be hoped for, was, early in our work, stricken down by severe sickness, from which he has not entirely recovered. All along, this committee have had the sympathy and co-operation of the entire board of directors, who deserve and must receive the sincere thanks of the membership of the Congregational churches throughout the land, for their gratuitous services and liberal gifts to secure this Congregational House. They may justly felicitate themselves upon the pleasing success already realized, and which you to-day can both see and enjoy.

I rejoice that our good mother, Congregationalism, who placed her foot upon this identical rock two hundred and fifty-two years ago, and has not had from that time to this a spot on earth she could call her own, at last has a *home.* She has deserved better of those to whom she committed, and for whom she has done, so much. Long has there been a great need of such a structure, embracing her history, and illustrating her principles and polity, "forming a centre of patriotic and religious reminiscence for New England, and for all the descendants of the Pilgrims, the shrine to which those who revere the memory of the great and the good and the learned of past ages might repair."

I rejoice that, as a branch of the great Christian family, we have now a centre of correspondence here, answering to the important position the Congregational churches have been called of God to occupy in the Christian world. It may not be apparent to you how this strong statement can be justified. But, for a moment, see what an amount of original, spirited, and valuable religious reading will issue from this building weekly, monthly, quarterly, annually. "The Congregationalist," among the best, if not the very best religious paper in the country, — and will, doubtless, be improved, when in its new and enlarged quarters here, — will go forth twenty-seven thousand strong every seven days. "The Well-Spring," our children's overflowing fountain, will divide itself into forty thousand little streamlets every week, running every whither. "The Missionary Herald," confessedly the ablest missionary periodical in our language, will greet its readers with its thirty thousand copies every month. "Life and Light for Woman," ten thousand copies, and "Echoes from Light and Life," eight thousand copies, will go every month. "The Advocate of Peace," forty-five hundred, and "Angel of Peace," ten thousand copies, twelve times told every year. "The Congregational Quarterly," two thousand copies every three months, a periodical too valuable and important not to be more widely circulated and better appreciated. Of these various issues alone there will be sent, in every direction, four millions two hundred and thirty-six thousand copies annually. And besides these, there will be the continuous issues of the Congregational Publishing Society, in volumes, tracts, leaflets, etc., — the Home Missionary for New England, the annual reports of all these societies; also, appeals, circulars, and letters, beyond computation, from all these rooms, reaching every part of the known world, so that you may be assured more that is of value to the world will go from this building, and more will be received in response that the friends of evangelization will want to know, than from and to any other thirteen thousand and three hundred square feet of earth to be found upon its surface. This house will be a centre of correspondence indeed, — a light, a city set upon a hill.

I rejoice that our ministers have a place where they can meet at their pleasure, and feel they have a right to be. Long has such a place been very much needed for this purpose. The pastors' meeting, as it is called, has been "carted" from room to room, begging or hiring its limited privileges, but having no permanent abiding place. Captain Robert Keayne set apart, in his will of 1653, a small sum to provide "a room for the elders to meet in and confer together when they have occasion to come to town for any such ends, as I perceive they have many." This was wise; and had his benevolent intentions been executed, the Congregational ministry of Boston, and the region round about, would have been greatly helped. At length the boon is vouchsafed, and these pleasant rooms are now at their disposal.

I rejoice that our churches have, at last, dared to lift up their banner to public view; that they are beginning to recognize the right and privilege of being known, and of calling themselves by their own name, without apology; that they are now willing to confess to a family relationship that will justify the erection of this structure as a symbol of their polity and principles; while, by priority of possession and means, if for no other reasons, they might long ago have taken advantage of such an essential help for every good work; yet, as a matter of fact, they have been the last in the brotherhood of Evangelical churches to build for themselves a family house. We may well take heart and give thanks, to-day, that at length we shall be able to point to one spot where Congregationalism can be found, — where its history may be learned, and its moral and Christian forces can be made more available and efficient. Upon this plain, simple, substantial, and imposing structure, the passer-by may look as a memorial of, and a living monument to, the founders of our churches, — to the men who laid the groundwork of our free civil institutions, — upon this building they may look as an expression of our appreciation of the great work these fathers performed, and of our estimate of the value of the glorious inheritance they so freely bequeathed to us.

I rejoice that our benevolent societies, having offices in this city, are now brought together under one roof, — thus greatly subserving the convenience of their constituency. Their work is *one* work; neither of these great agencies can dispense with either. The missionary societies must have missionaries; and to educate these, we must have literary institutions; and poor, pious students must be helped into the ministry or never reach it; and the feeble, struggling church, to become self-supporting, and hence a power for good, must have its sanctuary; and thus each of these great benevolences is inseparably interlocked with, and supplements, every other; and why should they not be brought into more intimate relationship as co-workers in a common cause? The more closely we can unite them, the more cordially will they affiliate, and so become more and more mutual helpers. Hitherto I have been in the habit of taking contributions for all these organizations, to accommodate the treasurers or pastors of out-of-town churches, to save them the necessity of losing their home-train or carrying back their money,—and I have paid them over,—not always to my convenience. Hereafter, if any society fails "to put in its appearance" here, where all belong, its intended contribution, left with me, *may* fail to reach its destination.

I rejoice that we have, at least, the shell of a fire-proof Library; the beginning of the beginning is secured. The gathering and preserving a Congregational Library for use was a primary object of this organization, and it has never been lost sight of in the somewhat more complex character of the work we have inaugurated. Indeed, the further we have gone, the more this primal object has risen in importance. It is believed we now have the best collection of books, pamphlets, and sermons, which state and illustrate our principles and polity, to be found in any public library in our country; and there waits the completion of our fire-proof building, the best private library in these same particulars known to me, the life-work of a most capable, indefatigable, and successful searcher after original papers, documents, and mementos of the first settlers of New England, — an invaluable collection, — to be gratuitously added to ours if we finish in season to secure it. These, together, would make this, unquestionably, the best Congregational Library in the world. May God, in infinite mercy, put it into the heart or hearts of some noble giver or givers to place the indispensable twenty-five thousand dollars in our hands to finish, at once, what we have here so well begun! Besides this waiting gift, there is another most carefully-selected theological library, the dying bequest of one of our ablest divines, now in the hands of his widow, also waiting the safe place here for its ultimate deposit. Besides these, there are other similar valuables known to me, that will be ours only when this so much needed Library building is ready for their reception. A treasure so valuable and so nearly in possession ought not, *must* not, be allowed to elude us.

I rejoice that now we are in a position, as never before, to do more and more effective work for the conversion of the world to Christ. Our working forces are brought together; our different channels of Christian labor are found to be in parallels and not at angles. We are in more favorable circumstances to know each other, and so increase brotherly love, and strengthen the bonds of Christian fellowship. Thus shall we be more and more mutual helpers in the Christian life, and so honor Christ. This house is Christ's house. It was begun in His name, and it has thus far been completed by His favor, and for His glory we hope soon to bring the top-stone with shoutings, crying, " Grace, grace unto it ! "

---

## REV. H. M. DEXTER, D. D.,

PRESENTED a part of a hewn stone window-cap taken by himself from the ruins of the old Manor House at Scrooby, in which — while it was occupied by William Brewster — the Mayflower church was cradled. He exhibited also one of the rudely-carved oaken beams from the wooden ceiling of the little chapel of the Manor House, which beam, in his opinion, was over the heads of the little company when they covenanted together "to walk in all His ways made known or to be made known to them, at whatever cost, the Lord assisting them."

## TIMOTHY GORDON, M. D.

If my name had not been announced among those who were expected to make "brief remarks," I certainly should not attempt to address you. And had I known before I left home that it was thus inserted, I should not have been here at all.

But as my friend, Mr. Langworthy, whom I never saw until I came into the building to-day, took me so cordially by the hand, with the pleasant expression, "I am glad to see you," which reminded me of my old friend, Dr. James Jackson, of this city, who, at a meeting of the Massachusetts Medical Society, took me by the hand, in the same felicitous manner, saying, "We must all be friends to-day, whether we have had a formal introduction or not," — so I feel we are all friends here to-day.

I think I stand in rather an unenviable position, without any opportunity to make preparation.

"Brief remarks." I think that is wise so far as it refers to me, because it must be a relief to the audience.

But I am here only to identify the genuineness of this piece of rock. Allow me here to correct one or two misstatements. I am not the Treasurer of the

Pilgrim Society, and never have been,— Isaac N. Stoddard, Esq., is the Treasurer, — and that this piece of rock is not the gift of myself alone. I stated to the Vice-President and to several of the Trustees, that it was desirable that a piece of the rock on which the Pilgrims landed should occupy some suitable place in the Congregational House in prospect of being erected. They all very generously told me to select such a piece as I thought proper, and present it; and this is the result. I supposed the piece of rock would occupy some conspicuous place on the front, or in some suit able "niche," and hope it will eventually be so. If I had known that it was to be placed in the library, I should have selected a differently-shaped piece much less in size.

I can assure you that it is a part of the rock upon which the Pilgrim fathers and mothers first landed in Plymouth in 1620. I saw it broken from that rock, and have been its custodian more than twelve years, with all that was taken from it at the time of laying the foundation of the present canopy which now covers its entire surface. At that time it was raised from its bed, and portions split off, to admit the corner-stones of the canopy to occupy their proper positions. The largest part then taken off has been disposed of, the avails of which have been paid towards finishing the canopy and the grounds surrounding it. And this piece, which is now presented to the Congregational House, is fully one tenth of all that is left, which was taken off at the time it was raised. As it is now placed no more can be taken from it. It is now very valuable; is sought after for jewelry, being susceptible of a beautiful finish.

The Pilgrim Society would be glad to have one hundred persons give in their names to become members, which would furnish five hundred dollars to help build a flight of stone steps, in ascending "Coles' Hill" from the canopy. I think it is very proper that these two relics of antiquity should be placed side by side,—the stone from Scrooby, the starting-point of the Pilgrims, who went out, not knowing whither they went, guided by an unseen hand, across the ocean to this very Plymouth Rock, leaving an imaginary bright and luminous pathway which will never be obliterated.

---

## GOV. WASHBURN'S REMARKS.

Mr. President, Ladies and Gentlemen:—I am happy to be present on this most interesting occasion. For the first time we are gathered in a building that we may call our own, a building belonging to the

Congregationalists of the country, set apart for their special uses and as their home. I hope no mere sectarian idea will ever cause us to forget that Christianity is above all sects; and yet I do not deny that I have a strong feeling of satisfaction that we are permitted, as a denomination, to occupy this house.

Coming to this city mostly unacquainted with you, the Congregational Club opened its doors and welcomed me to its gatherings. I have enjoyed the fellowship of its members and the benefit of their counsels, and I wish here and now to return my thanks to them for their kindness. But notwithstanding their courtesy and generosity, I confess that I have felt myself in some sense an interloper. I have been as one treading on foreign ground. But I shall not be troubled in that way any longer. For I feel now very much like the boy of whom you have read, who was examining that beautiful little ship, the Morning Star, which has been an instrument of so much good to millions in foreign lands, when one of the hands on the vessel treated him roughly and ordered him to leave the deck. He replied, "I shall not do it; I am a stockholder in this ship; I have my certificate of stock; you cannot deprive me of my rights." I recollect that soon after the enterprise to secure this building was entered upon, I was visited in the western part of the State by your agent, and contributed my mite towards the fund required, and hence became a stockholder, and thus have my rights here to-day. And I am specially gratified that I have an opportunity now to welcome the members of the Congregational Club to our rooms.

We have rallying points for clubs and associations on every hand, — one or more on nearly every important street in the city. There is power in combination. The good men and women whom I see before me to-day believe in unity of action. But under whatever banner we enlist, and whatever the name thereon inscribed, we should not forget that the value of our efforts will be measured by the good we accomplish. This noble building, to-day dedicated to the uses of Congregationalism, is valuable just in proportion as it enables those who gather here to devise and carry out plans for the benefit of mankind. May it prove a source from which will flow influences calculated to elevate and ennoble all ranks and classes of society! May light and warmth radiate from this centre to every quarter of the globe, till the principles of Christianity are everywhere triumphant!

## HON. EMORY WASHBURN.

Mr. Washburn said that he inferred, from being called upon to speak on this occasion, while surrounded by such a brilliant constellation of clerical talent, that he was expected to say a word of our Puritan ancestors in their character as legislators. The subject was especially suited to the occasion, since nothing was a surer test of the character, intelligence, and habits of thought of a people than their laws. We had only to trace these to read the history of a nation, and of the moral and social changes through which it has passed, which have found expression in the legislation in which they have been recorded. It is through her laws that a nation gives us an insight into her inner life, of which we gain little by the ordinary events which are recorded in history. This is especially true of the Puritans of Massachusetts, who have left a faithful record of their entire legislation under the colony charter, without concealing or coloring a thought or an action. And though this has supplied a text for many a third-rate politician, whose claim to smartness seems to have rested mainly upon the degree of severity with which he has flippantly denounced the bigotry and intolerance of the Puritans, Mr. Washburn would venture to affirm that a wiser or more liberal policy never characterized the legislation of any people than marked the laws which those same Puritans adopted for the growth and development of what they came here to found,— a Christian Commonwealth.

In the few moments allotted to him, it would be impossible to illustrate this remark by reciting any number of the more remarkable of those laws; but he would venture to allude to one, which has been so often referred to as evidence of the narrow and sectarian zeal of the early founders of the colony. The one he had in mind related to requiring all freemen to be members of some church, thus making church-membership a qualification as a voter. How often had they heard this "union of church and state," this "bigoted exclusiveness" in the election of their officers, made the ground of obloquy and reproach upon these men, by orators and critics who, probably, never stopped to ask why such a law was adopted. A law is wise and liberal, or otherwise, according as it is suited to the condition of the people for whom it is made. What, then, was the condition of the Massachusetts colony when that law was passed? It bears date May, 1631, less than one year after the government had been organized under Winthrop, and before it had become settled and established. The system under the charter was wellnigh a pure democracy. Every freeman of the colony had a right, and for some years after its founding exercised it, to take a part in its administration, by choosing officers, admitting freemen, and administering justice in popular assemblies, where all came together and acted by majorities. The colony had left many active and determined enemies at home, ready to seize upon any pretence for depriving it of its free charter. In the planting of all new colonies there is a class of restless and uneasy spirits who, having nothing to lose, are ready to find their way into the new settlements as they are formed, with a view to promote their own ends, or to escape the restraints of salutary laws. There were such in and around the Massachusetts colony from the first. In the hands of their enemies, or unprincipled men, the government was not safe a moment. The purposes for which they had come here would be defeated, and the sacrifices to which they had been subjected would be wholly lost to their posterity as well as to themselves. They sought, therefore, to check such intruders, by prescribing some safeguard in the form of a qualification to the becoming a freeman. And why did they do it? They have told us in the language of the act itself: "To the end, the Body of the Commons may be *preserved* honest and good men." Here was the reason. The peace and good order ot the state, — not a word said of giving power to the church. Indeed, there was no one church known. The churches were organizations, independent of each other, and independent of the state. So far from aiming to confer power upon the church as a body, we find a statute in 1641 expressly declaring that church censures should not affect the civil rights of any one.

But to test the character and spirit of these legislators, and the working of this restrictive law, what evidence do we find in the legislation which followed? In 1641, the members of the General Court, chosen by such electors as these, adopted and published to the world, forty-one years before the English Bill of Rights had been declared, a "Body of Liberties," which was drawn up by a Congregational minister, for, as they say, "the free fruition of such liberties, immunities, and privileges as humanity, civility, and Christianity call for, as dear to every man in his place and proportion, without impeachment and infringement." And, in that Body of Liberties, we find the memorable declaration, that "there shall never be any bond slavery" amongst them, except in the cases, in effect, which were forced upon them by the mother country.

So that in fact there never was, from that day, a native-born slave, lawfully held as such in Massachusetts. And in this they did all they were permitted to do as colonists, in abolishing slavery, and they made a further public declaration of their condemnation of the institution, by securing to such as they could not set free, "all the liberties and Christian usages which the law of God, established in Israel, doth morally require."

Mr. W. said his time would allow him to refer to only one more subject, that of free schools. In 1642, the representatives of this body of freemen enjoined upon the towns to provide education for every child within their jurisdiction. And, in 1647, a law was passed making the support of schools compulsory, and education therein *free* to *all.* These bigoted, narrow-minded, intolerant men, of their own motion, inaugurated a system of free schools, in which they anticipated England by more than two hundred years, which struck a fatal blow to everything like class or denominational distinction under a free government. It not only assumed that all were free and equal, but it provided, at the public charge, the means by which all might become so, if they would. Neither rank, nor sex, nor color was any longer to be a barrier to the refining and elevating influence of education, or to the sharing of power, which comes from the possession of intelligence and culture.

With such laws as these, it is idle to charge upon the men of that day, that they had a thought of building up in the community a system which was to favor church members beyond any other class of citizens. They give in their own language the reason why they enacted the law of 1647, while they repeat their ever-conscious reliance upon that Providence which had thus far guided and watched over them: "That learning be not buried in the graves of our forefathers, in *church and commonwealth*, — the Lord assisting our endeavors."

If any one would follow the course of legislation of the Puritans under the colony charter, he would find, with all there was to criticise, a noble consistency in the same high aims and purposes of founding and building up a Christian commonwealth, in which they had little to guide them but their Bibles, and their own sense of what were the rights and duties of a free people. And proud as we might be of Massachusetts in her history, there was no period of her annals which reflects higher honor upon the men who took the lead in her affairs, than that during which the Puritans directed her legislation. If they were bigoted, it was the fault of the age in which they lived. Their own spontaneous action was all in favor of elevating and improving the condition of their fellow-men. Their bigotry expended itself in trying to preserve their fellow-citizens "honest and good men." And if that is *bigotry*, the more a people have of it the better.

If bigotry is a disease in the body politic, and it takes that turn, people might almost pray that it might become epidemic, and "break out" with new and fresh vigor, outside of Massachusetts as well as within it, and spread till it reached the capital itself, and the men who are gathered there.

---

## PROF. EDWARDS A. PARK

Was to have delivered the last of the brief addresses. Being obliged to leave before he could secure his opportunity, under urgent importunity he has sent the following letter: —

REV. ISAAC P. LANGWORTHY:

DEAR SIR: If I had made the speech I was designing to make at the dedication of the Congregational House, I should have named several particulars in which the House is fitted to preserve the spirit of ancient Congregationalism, and should have narrated a few of the proceedings which resulted in the formation of the Society which you have served so long and so well. In this letter I will omit the remarks which

I had intended to make on the fitnesses of the Congregational House, and will narrate, more minutely than I had intended in my speech to detail, some incidents connected with the inception of the Society whose treasure of books is to enrich the House.

On the fifth of October, 1843, I made my first visit to the Red Cross Library, the great library of the dissenters, in the city of London. I was deeply impressed by the portraits which adorned the walls of the edifice, and by the old and rare books which filled its shelves. Here were the portrait of John Milton, and the first edition of his Paradise Lost; and not far from the edifice was the home of the blind poet. This library, of thirty thousand volumes; these portraits, more than eighty in number, of such men as Bates, Baxter, Cartwright, Caryl, Charnock, Flavel, Matthew Henry, John Howe, Manton, Perkins, Ridgeley, Watts, and men of kindred spirit, — had long engaged the interest of Prof. B. B. Edwards; and in the winter of 1843–4, we both became fully convinced that a library and a portrait gallery similar to those in Red Cross Street, London, might be established in New England. After frequent conversations with each other, the plan appeared so feasible that we agreed to propose it to several clergymen in and near Boston. I remember that on the twenty-fourth of May, 1844, I had a lengthened interview with Rev. William M. Rogers, and called his attention to a remark which I had intended to make in a sermon before the Pastoral Association of Massachusetts. The sermon was delivered on the twenty-eighth of May, and printed in the following month. The remark was: " Let us establish in this city of the Pilgrims, a Pilgrim Hall, that shall contain the writings of our fathers, and of our brethren, and of our successors, and let its walls preserve the portraits of our Cottons, and our Mathers, and our Hookers, and our Emmonses, and our Paysons, and our Hallocks, and our Beechers."

Prof. Edwards desired several persons travelling in Europe to make a thorough examination of the Red Cross Library, and to publish a description of it. When he embarked for Europe in 1846, he determined to perform this work himself. He printed his essay on the library in August, 1847. The essay is found in the Bibliotheca Sacra, Vol. IV, pp. 582–598, and also in his Memoir, pp. 256–276. In this suggestive article, he proposes the establishment of a Puritan Library and Museum "in some one of the large cities of New England, the capital, for example." To the question : " What departments and branches should such a library and museum include," he answers, First: It should include books, pamphlets, and periodicals published by the Puritans in England and in this country; the old and small newspapers, the "Apologies," "De fences," "Rejoinders," "Appeals," "Statements," which illustrate the minute history of the Puritans and the Pilgrims. Secondly: The library should gather together the manuscripts of our old divines, the "many precious papers not now known to exist, utterly neglected, mouldering in chests or in garrets, constantly exposed to destruction," etc. Thirdly: There should be collected in the library and museum original por traits, prints, engravings, busts of the eminent men who have adorned our churches. Fourthly: The museum should contain "miscellaneous memorials, cherished articles employed in the studies and in the labors of distinguished men, characteristic remembrancers, even should they be small and in themselves of little value." The reasons he assigns for establishing such a library and museum are the following: —

First: The establishment "would form a centre for patriotic and religious reminiscence for New England and for all the descendants of the Pilgrims." Secondly: It "would constitute an interesting memorial of the theological and literary labors" of our New-England fathers. Thirdly: It would be one means of perpetuating their religious principles and usages. Fourthly: It "would be of inestimable service to our future civil and ecclesiastical historians." Fifthly: It "would tend to promote brotherly feelings among the descendants of the Puritans." Sixthly: It "would exert a favorable influence on the character of the sermons and other works which may hereafter be published by our clergymen." Seventhly: It "would ensure the preservation of valuable documents and curiosities which will otherwise be lost," and would thus be of great historical worth.

This essay of Prof. Edwards attracted the notice of some opulent laymen. Hon. Samuel T. Armstrong exerted himself in favor of the plan, and in his last conversation with Mr. Edwards, expressed his hope and belief that the Old South Church of Boston would aid the enterprise liberally. (Memoir of Prof. Edwards, p. 271.) He also thought that the valuable library of Dr. Prince might be connected in some way with the general library proposed in the essay.

After numerous consultations with clergymen and laymen, a plan was formed for the establishment of a Society which would collect the books and the portraits of the fathers, and also devote itself to the advancement of theological science. It was proposed that the Society should consist of three sections,— one devoted to biblical philology, another to ecclesiastical history, and another to theological doctrine. Essays were to be read before each of these sections, and afterwards published. Branches of the Society were to be formed in various parts of the country, and the results of their studies communicated to the general Society. This plan was an organized form of conducting such literary exercises, as in a less methodical way are now conducted by some theological clubs. The society was to be, and was familiarly called, an Academy of Theological Science.

Some advocates of the plan desired that this Theological Association or Academy should have its library, or at least its centre of operations, in Andover rather than in Boston, and that the more prominent essays written for it should be read at the Andover anniversary, and should take the place of the annual sermon before the alumni. Several of these friends did not believe that the plan could be executed without reviving an old "odium theologicum," and they consequently recommended a further delay. Two parties had been for a long time contending in New England under the leadership of two divines, of whom it has been said that their names differed from each other in only a single letter, and their theological systems differed in such minute particulars that not a single partisan of either system could state the particulars in such a form as would meet the approval of the two divines themselves. At length, however, it was determined to try the experiment. Prof. Edwards and myself invited two clergymen to meet us on the twenty-second of November, 1850. Of the clergymen invited, one was Rev. (now Dr.) William I. Budington, a supposed representative of the theological party led by the divine who had an "a" in his name, and the other clergyman was Rev. (afterwards Dr.) Alexander McClure, a supposed representative of the party led by the divine who had no "a" in his name.

The meeting was held in my house at two o'clock in the afternoon. It was enlivened by the wit of Dr. McClure, cheered by the genial manners of Dr. Budington, and rendered memorable by the modest and earnest words of Prof. Edwards. We formed ourselves into a committee of four, and discussed the principles to be incorporated into the constitution of the society. The constitution was afterwards somewhat modified by Drs. McClure and Budington, and on the eighteenth of December they reported that their draft was finished, and sent to Prof. Edwards and myself a copy of it. On the fifth of February, 1851, they read their constitution to a company consisting of "Rev. Messrs. Albro, Pomeroy, Thompson, Tappan, Treat, Richards, Alvord, Higgins, Foster, Jenks, Anderson, J. S. Clark, Riddel, Cushing, Waterbury, and Peck." The constitution was formally adopted, and the first officers of the Society were elected at an adjourned meeting, Feb. 12, 1851.

Yours truly,

EDWARDS A. PARK.

ANDOVER THEOLOGICAL SEMINARY, May 3, 1873.

# MAP.

THE little map below — for which we are indebted to the proprietors of the "Congregationalist" — will give our friends a correct idea of the relative location of the Congregational House and of its excellent surroundings.

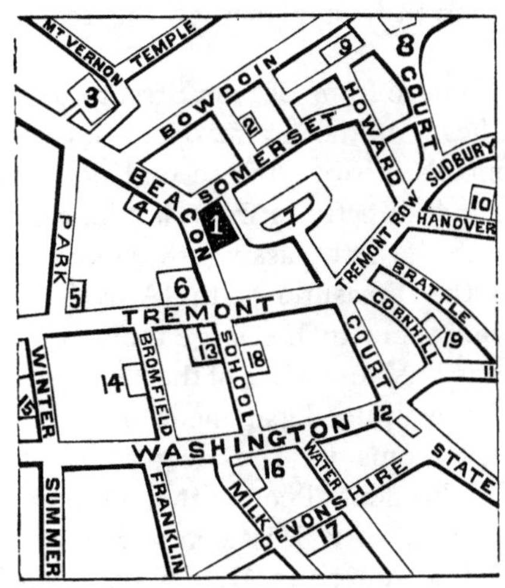


## DESCRIPTION OF MAP.

1. CONGREGATIONAL HOUSE.
2. MOUNT VERNON CHURCH.
3. STATE HOUSE.
4. ATHENÆUM.
5. PARK STREET CHURCH.
6. TREMONT HOUSE.
7. PEMBERTON SQUARE.
8. BOWDOIN SQUARE.
9. REVERE HOUSE.
10. AMERICAN HOUSE.
11. DOCK SQUARE.
12. OLD STATE HOUSE.
13. PARKER HOUSE.
14. WESLEYAN HALL.
15. 40 WINTER STREET.
16. OLD SOUTH CHURCH.
17. NEW POST OFFICE BUILDING.
18. CITY HALL.

## DESCRIPTION OF THE BUILDING.

THE engraving opposite the title-page gives a fair view of the Congregational House as seen by one coming down Beacon Street. It has a frontage of one hundred and three feet on Beacon Street, and a side view of ninety-three feet on Somerset Street. The entrances from each street are directly under the bay-windows as seen on this elevation. The monitor roof peering above its surroundings, covers the Library building, whose exact relations to the other parts of the house can be readily perceived by a glance at the second-floor plan inserted here.

On entering the house from Beacon Street, the first door on the right, at the head of the stairs, opens into the beautiful rooms of the Woman's Board ; the second door leads to the Librarian's room, and directly in front is the entrance to the Library ; turning to the left, passing three large parlors, you reach the room of the Treasurer of the A. B. C. F. M. ; turning to the right, you come to the large room occupied by his clerks ; thence to the business office of the "Congregationalist" on the left, and its mailing department on the right. The third floor furnishes rooms for the Secretaries of the Board, editor of "Herald," Prudential committee, museum, clerk and copyists of the Board, City Missionary Society, American Congregational Union, American Missionary Association, and Massachusetts Home Missionary Society. The fourth floor has Pilgrim Hall, general committee and ministerial conference room, — which, together, have the capacity of seating six hundred persons, — the American Peace Society, editors of the "Congregationalist," and two large rooms which are temporarily occupied with a part of the Congregational Library. The fifth floor, fronting on Somerset Street, is occupied by Thomas Todd, Esq., for composition and printing. The janitor lives in well-finished rooms in the attic of what was the Gardner House. The Congregational Publishing Society occupies the store on the corner of Beacon and Somerset Streets, and the two rooms upon the first floor fronting on Somerset Street are the office of the "Missionary Herald," and the packing-room of the American Board.

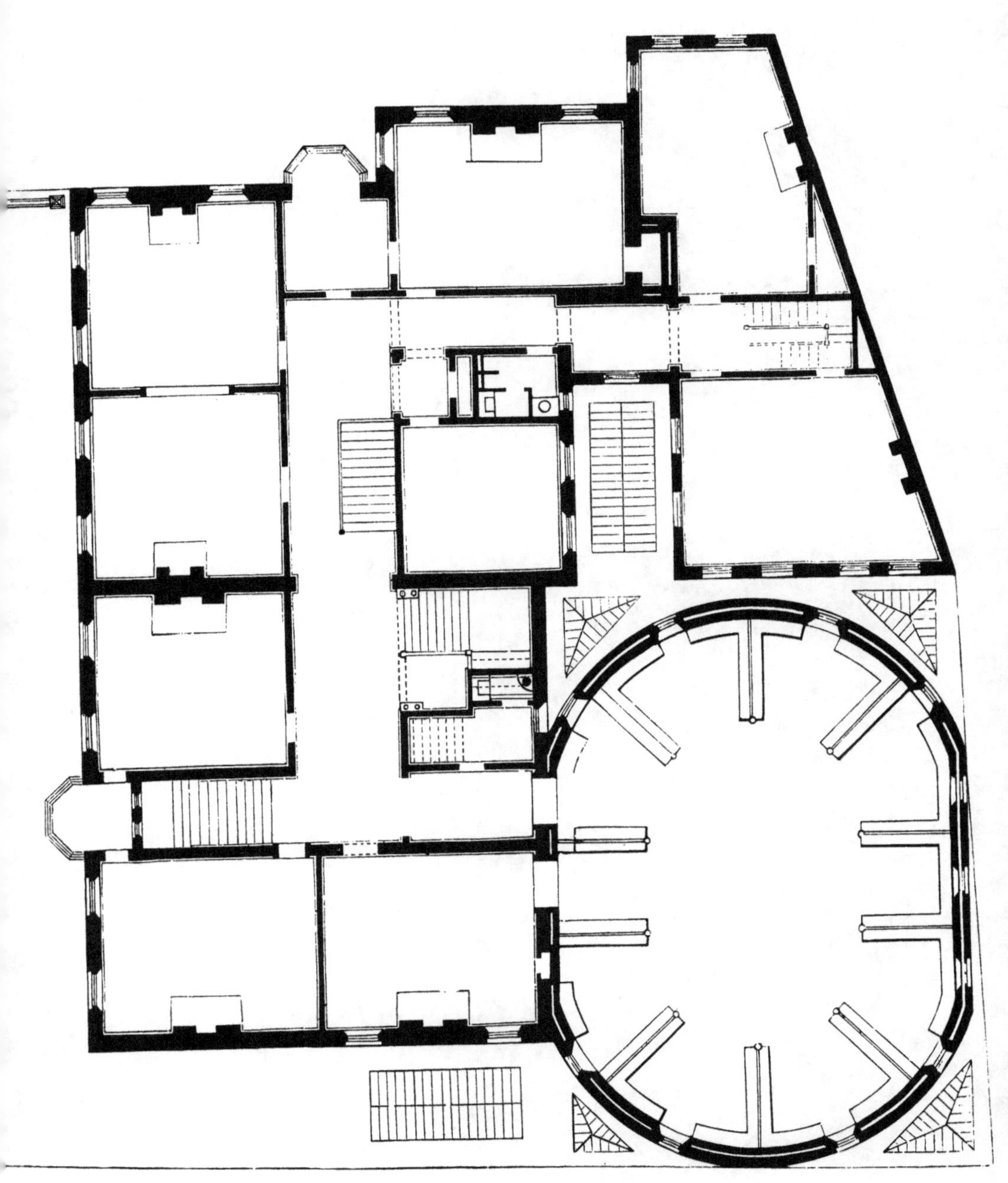

# THE AMERICAN

# CONGREGATIONAL ASSOCIATION.

## A BRIEF HISTORICAL SKETCH.

THE organization, which is here but merely outlined, came into existence from the convictions and efforts of a number of interested men. They seem to have been simultaneously impressed with the importance of saving whatever was still within the possible reach of the writings and memorials of the early settlers of this country. The first public discussion of the subject, of recent date, was by Prof. Bela B. Edwards, of Andover, Mass., in an able article in the August number of the "Bibliotheca Sacra," 1847, in which — making the Dr. Williams' Library of London the basis — he forcibly urged the importance and practicability of a public library of books, pamphlets, manuscripts, and whatever else would serve to illustrate the Pilgrim and Puritan history and New-England theology.

Previously to this, however, there had been not a little conversation and planning with reference to this same end. Some persons now living will recall earnest suggestions and expressions of deep interest, in this behalf, from the late Rev. William M. Rogers, also from the Rev. Joseph S. Clark, Rev. Drs. Anderson and Felt, and some others. The donor of the imperfect copy of Eliot's Bible remembers perfectly an appeal from Mr. Rogers for that book, saying, "You must let me have it, or give it to the Congregational Library which we must have." This was in 1843 or 1844. But this sporadic interest took no especial form until the winter of 1851, when Prof. Edwards, in consultation with Prof. E. A. Park, D. D., invited the Rev. Wm. Ives Budington, then of Charlestown, now of Brooklyn, N. Y., and the late Rev. A. W. McClure, then of Malden, to an interview with them on this subject at Andover. As one of the immediate results of that conference, a meeting was called at the rooms of the American Education Society, 15 Cornhill, in Boston, and was held February 5, 1851, at 10 o'clock, A. M., at which the following named clergymen were present: the Rev. Messrs. John A. Albro, D. D., Jared B. Waterbury, D. D., Rufus Anderson, D. D., Nehemiah Adams, D. D., Edward Beecher, D. D., Frederick T. Perkins, Samuel H. Riddel, Alexander W. McClure, George Richards, Joseph S. Clark, William A. Stearns, S. Hale Higgins, Christopher Cushing, William C. Foster, John W. Alvord, and Wm. Ives Budington. The Rev. Dr. Anderson was invited to preside, and the Rev. Mr. Budington to officiate as scribe. The minutes continue: "After prayer for divine guidance, and a free interchange of views, it was unanimously voted that, in the judgment of this meeting, it is *expedient* to form a society for the establishment of a Congregational Library, and the cultivation of theological science." A committee was appointed, consisting of the Rev. Messrs. McClure, Anderson, Albro, Beecher, and Budington, to take the subject into consideration, and report a constitution at the next meeting, to be holden at the same place on the following Tuesday, at ten o'clock, A. M. . At that meeting there were present the Rev. Messrs. Albro, Pomeroy, Thompson, Tappan, Treat, Richards, Alvord, Foster, Higgins, Jenks, McClure, Anderson, Clark, Riddel, Cushing, Waterbury, and Budington. The constitution was presented, discussed, and finally, after numerous amendments, was adopted, and the following officers were chosen by ballot: Rev. J. A. Albro,

President; Rev. Geo. W. Blagden, Vice-President; Rev. Wm. Ives Budington, Secretary; Rev. A. W. McClure, Treasurer; and Rev. Wm. Jenks, D. D., Librarian. Encouraged by the interest taken in these incipient movements by the pastor, Rev. Mr Blagden, and the Hon. Samuel T. Armstrong, both of the Old South Church, measures were immediately adopted to direct, as far as possible, the efforts of this Association, so as to secure the benefits of the Prince Library, under the care of the deacons of that church. Arrangements were made for future meetings at the rooms of that library, in Spring Lane Chapel, and permission was given to add a suitable book-case for the preservation and use of the first fruits of the Association.

The Association met in the Old South Chapel, Spring Lane, November 19, 1851, and continued to hold its regular and special meetings there until May 25, 1853, when it was reorganized and became a new body. No very decided efforts seem to have been made to create a library during this period. From the written catalogue of Dr. Jenks, handed over to his successor, there were but fifty-six books and pamphlets, all told, and forty-three of these were the gifts of two men, viz.: twenty-three by J. Wingate Thornton, Esq., of Boston, and twenty by the Rev. A. W. McClure, of Malden. The meetings of the Association had been held monthly, except in July, August, and September, and were devoted mostly to essays and discussions upon historical, ecclesiastical, and theological subjects.

The records of the Association, which now came into the careful and accurate hands of the Rev. Joseph S. Clark, D. D., have the following minutes touching this change in its form: "After various modifications in the working of the system for the space of two years, it became evident, that, with some other modifications, the essential *idea* of the Association was capable of indefinite expansion, and was quite too important to be restrained within the present sphere of its development.

Accordingly, the subject of an extended organization was given in charge to a committee consisting of the Rev. Messrs. Parsons Cooke, D. D., Rufus Anderson, D. D., Edward Beecher, D. D., Samuel M. Worcester, D. D., A. C. Thompson, Nehemiah Adams, D. D., and Sewall Harding. Their report was made to a full meeting of the body on the 19th of May, 1853; and after a thorough discussion and revision, it was unanimously adopted, and became the basis of a new and enlarged organization (retaining the same name), which, with great unanimity, was formed in the Old South Chapel on the 25th day of May, 1853, in the midst of a large assembly of Congregational ministers and laymen, drawn together from all the New-England States and from other parts of the land.

"Immediately after the organization was completed, and before the assembly had dispersed, a committee from the Pastoral Association of Massachusetts, who had been charged with that business, called a meeting of that body, and reported a resolution, which was unanimously adopted, to the effect that the Pastoral Association do now merge itself in the Congregational Library Association, and declare its own organization dissolved,—thus nationalizing (not surrendering) the essential objects of its existence, and pursuing them henceforth in company with the great family of Congregational pastors and church members throughout the land.

"Subsequently the members of the original organization (about twenty-five in all) met, and, after a formal transfer of their records and property, unanimously voted to merge their Congregational Library Association into the newly-formed body of the same name, and then declared the organization dissolved."

The second article of the new constitution was as follows: "The object of this Association shall be to found and perpetuate a Library of Books, Pamphlets, and Manuscripts, and a collection of Portraits, and whatever else shall serve to illustrate Puritan History, and promote the general interests of Congregationalism." The officers then chosen by ballot were: Rev. William T. Dwight, D. D., of Portland, Me., President, with a long list of Vice-Presidents; for Directors, Rev. Parsons Cooke, D. D., Rev. Samuel M. Worcester, D. D., Rev. Sewall Harding, Rev. Augustus C. Thompson, Rev. Rufus Anderson, D. D., Julius A. Palmer, Esq.; for Corresponding Secretary, Rev. Joseph S. Clark; Recording Secretary, Rev. Samuel H. Riddel; Librarian, Rev. Joseph B. Felt, D. D.; for Treasurer, Alpheus Hardy, Esq.

An application was now made to the legislature for a charter, which was granted April 12, 1854, and has, several times since, been amended, — changing the name, and giving the privilege of holding real and personal estate to the amount of seven hundred and fifty thousand dollars.

The Association was now prepared to make itself an influence for good, and began at once to discuss the subject of erecting "a large and costly edifice," and that on the ground "that it will be better economy than a small and cheap one." A suitable room for temporary use was rented in Tremont Temple, where the directors met for the first time, July 11, 1853.

The first definite action taken by the directors for the purchase of, or otherwise securing a suitable building for the purposes of the Association, was at their meeting, October 31, 1854, when Messrs. Hardy, Palmer, and Clark were appointed a committee "to find a suitable site."

At a special meeting held April 17, 1855, it was voted: "That it is expedient that immediate measures be taken by this Board to raise funds for the erection of such a building," — the Congregational House, — and the committee on "site" were instructed to make "all necessary arrangements" therefor. At the annual meeting, held May 29, 1855, the subject above named was fully presented, discussed, and unanimously indorsed; and the sum of $50,000 was recommended as the amount to be raised. The Rev. Dr. Clark decided to make a temporary effort to secure the required funds, having obtained consent of the executive committee of the Massachusetts Home Missionary Society, whose corresponding secretary he long had been, and immediately entered upon this work, securing subscriptions to the amount of nineteen hundred and seventy dollars from the directors present. November 24, 1856, the committee on site presented a recommendation of an estate on Tremont Street, fronting the Common, which was adopted ; and it was voted, "That immediate efforts be made to raise the funds for purchasing the said estate." The "appointment and selecting of an agent" was given to a special committee, with instructions "to confer with the Rev. I. P. Langworthy and his people, respecting his appointment to the agency." This failing, the committee secured the consent of the Rev. Dr. Clark to continue in this service, according to their previous arrangements with him.

At a meeting held May 6, 1857, it being found impossible to secure the requisite funds for the purchase of the estate on Tremont Street, and "the late Judge Jackson estate on Chauncy Street being offered on more favorable terms," it was purchased for the sum of twenty-five thousand dollars, the next day. June 28, 1857, a committee reported that arrangements had been made with the Rev. Dr. Clark to become the financial agent of the Association.

From the beginning of his peculiarly skillful and patiently-enduring efforts to raise funds for this object, he met with opposition where he might the least have expected it, and *indifference* all but everywhere. Thoroughly informed upon its chief bearings, and deeply convinced of its importance, he went forward amid repulses and cold shoulders, such as would have driven any but a man wholly in earnest from the field. It was so entirely a new thing, in modern times, for Congregationalists to do anything which could be called denominational, that not a few esteemed this movement a great mistake, if not a crime. By dint of unflinching perseverance, however, he succeeded in raising between eight and nine thousand dollars, a part of which was paid upon the Jackson estate, and the remainder upon necessary changes in fitting the building for occupancy. The library was moved to this building in the early summer of 1857. He continued to visit the churches and associations, soliciting funds and securing more or less books and pamphlets, until his lamented death, August 17th, 1861. For five months the late rebellious war had raged, and very little could be done in raising subscriptions or contributions. The want of that co-operation and sympathy which he had a right to expect, bore heavily upon his sensitive mind, and, by many it is believed, hastened his death. But those who survive him understand that he accomplished much more than he lived to see, opening the way, enlightening some of the ignorance and removing some of the prejudice which was so universal upon this simple question of proper denominational action. Thus, he was enabled to herald, if he did not assure, the success that has attended subsequent efforts.

The subject of issuing from the library rooms a monthly or quarterly periodical, answering, somewhat, to the character of the "American Quarterly Register," had been a long cherished idea with Dr. Clark, and was brought before his directors for discussion at their meeting of Jan. 28, 1858; and after due consideration, was referred to a committee to make further investigation and report. In the meantime, Drs. Dexter and Quint were maturing plans for starting a similar work, and on conferring with Dr. Clark, an arrangement was entered into for issuing the "Congregational Quarterly," the first number of which greeted its friends early in January, 1859. The Association, represented by Dr. C. and Rev. Drs. Dexter and Quint, were joint proprietors; and before the issue of the April number, the "American Congregational Union" merged its "Year Book" in the "Quarterly," and became, through its secretary, a fourth partner, and joint proprietor, of this now standard and much-needed periodical.

Dr. Clark contributed largely to its pages, labored faithfully to secure subscribers and send them their numbers until the close of his life. It continued to be issued from the rooms of the Association until the close of the fourteenth volume—1872—when the Association disposed of its interest to the other proprietors.

Immediately after the decease of Dr. Clark, the Rev. Isaac P. Langworthy, then corresponding secretary of the American Congregational Union, having his desk in the library, was requested to take the oversight of the building, and direction of the boy in charge; and at the next annual meeting, May 27, 1862, was appointed corresponding secretary and librarian; and by an amicable arrangement between the trustees of the Union and the directors of the Association, he was to receive two hundred dollars of his salary from the latter, for the care of the "boy" and the "building"; and no further service was expected, except the calling of the occasional meetings, and conducting the limited correspondence of the Association.

The library then contained three thousand six hundred and thirty-eight bound volumes, and about twenty thousand pamphlets. The books were arranged according to size and binding, the pamphlets in closets mostly unsorted. Dr. Clark was so familiar with all the books that he had little difficulty in finding any book desired, but to others the arrangement was not convenient. Being compelled, from need of funds, to rent the second story of the building, and hence to remove the library shelves one more flight up, advantage was taken of this occasion to separate all the duplicates, and so far as the limited room would allow, to arrange the books according to their subjects; and at the same time the three private libraries in charge were returned to their owners. This plan revealed more clearly the especial needs of the library, and the empty shelving made its own appeal to all visitors; and from that time to the present, the increase of the library has been quite rapid and valuable, when it is considered that the Association has never appropriated *one cent* of its funds to buy a book.

It is, however, but just to say that this great increase did not "*happen*," nor have books come in, one or two thousand volumes a year, of their own accord. There has been some forecasting and planning, but more begging and hard work. In the several issues of the "Quarterly," the librarian stated more or less of the immediate wants of the library of periodicals, minutes, and such like, to complete sets, and thus attention was called to the library, and valuable gifts were received.

On the Sabbath he was presenting his church-building work, stopping with the pastors, to whose libraries he always had access, and from whose houses he seldom returned without a full satchel, or a clever package of books or pamphlets, or both, or had a larger package, or box, or barrel, speedily to follow him by express. And in these trips he often found his way to the closets or attics of retired ministers, or of the descendants of ministers, from which valuable treasures for these shelves have been received. The heirs of deceased ministers, and of a number of distinguished laymen, have, on request, given a good, if not the larger part, of very valuable libraries. In these ways no inconsiderable number of duplicates were found to accumulate. These have served as a basis for very extensive exchanges with all the principal libraries for hundreds of miles around. By the sale of some duplicates and of waste paper carefully preserved for that purpose, and from some small gifts of friends, a thousand volumes, more or less, of the more rare and valuable books of the library have been purchased. Two hundred and nineteen dollars *for binding* have been appropriated from the treasury, and nothing more has come from the contributions of the churches to secure the more than FIFTEEN THOUSAND BOUND VOLUMES AND QUITE FIFTY THOUSAND PAMPHLETS now in the library. While many of these are of a somewhat miscellaneous character, and may at some future day be exchanged for others more nearly in the line of its specialties, yet it is believed to be entirely true that the mass of both volumes and pamphlets is just what is essential, and very many of them could not be easily reproduced. In securing the early and contemporaneous history of the Congregational churches of New England, and of the country, indeed, importunity and perseverance have been quite reasonably rewarded.

It should be said, further, that the efforts of the librarian have been stimulated in this particular direction, partly from the fact that the financial condition of the country did not justify especial appeals to the churches for building funds during a part of the period now referred to, and in part from the feeling so common, that the plan for a Congregational House was more ideal and fanciful than real and substantial; that it did not arise from any especial need, nor did it promise any especial, solid good. It came at length to be seen that there was gathered in this incipient library a substantial and valuable treasure, that absolutely needed just the structure proposed. And it is no baseless prediction to say, that when its now well-begun fire-proof building is complete, there will be here very soon thereafter, the best Congregational, ecclesiastical, historical, exegetical, and Biblical library in the country, and, in some of its features, the best in the world.

Earnest efforts were made in the spring of 1862, by the directors of this Association, to unite it with the American Congregational Union, — having the peculiar church-building work of the latter transferred to the former. The proposition was favorably and courteously entertained by a large majority of the trustees of the Union, but failed of a sanction by the members at their next annual meeting.

Early in 1864, the question of raising funds for the Congregational House was discussed at various meetings of the directors; and December 28th of that year, Henry Edwards, Esq., of this city, was appointed financial agent for Boston and vicinity. He entered upon this service without fee or reward, and accomplished much, both in removing prejudice and in securing reliable subscriptions. His extensive business acquaintance, as well as his gentlemanly bearing and admirable tact, gave him, in the circumstances, gratifying success. The amount required to make these subscriptions binding, however, was not secured. There seemed to be, nevertheless, an imperious necessity for pressing the matter of subscriptions at once, and the Rev. A. P. Marvin, of Winchendon, was engaged to give his whole time to this work for one year. He carefully and faithfully canvassed Boston and vicinity, and other cities of this State, and, to some extent, of other New-England States, presenting the subject on the Sabbath wherever he could, encountering, very generally, the same all but insurmountable indifferences and difficulties that had confronted his predecessors in the same line of effort. With wonderful patience and characteristic persistence, he went through his term of service, and continued it for five months afterwards, — securing the renewal of the most of the subscriptions that had been previously given to Mr. Edwards, bringing the whole sum up to the required fifty thousand dollars, — making the pledges binding, — the most of which were subsequently redeemed.

The directors were among the first to take active measures in relation to the calling of the National Council of 1865, and were represented at the preliminary meeting held in New York, November 16, 1864; and on the invitation of one of its directors, providentially present, that council was held at Boston. The objects of the Association were cordially commended by this council to the confidence and contributions of the churches.

During this year there was a careful revision of the Constitution and By-Laws, and some important changes were made; all of which were unanimously adopted at the next annual meeting of the Association, and in their essential features have remained as they are now published herewith.

The property on Chauncy Street was found to be appreciating in value, and yet was quite too limited to accommodate the increasing needs of the library, and the different benevolent societies that desired rooms in the Congregational House. It was voted, November 28, 1866, to sell the estate, and for this purpose an especial committee was appointed. The sale was soon after effected to Messrs. Jordan & Marsh, for fifty-seven thousand six hundred and eighty-four dollars. This relieved the embarrassments of the Association, so that on removing to 40 Winter Street, March 1st, 1867, there was on hand about sixty thousand dollars well invested, a library of six thousand and sixty bound volumes, and nearly thirty-thousand pamphlets.

Towards the close of the preceding year, arrangements were made with the Corresponding Secretary to give his whole time to the work of the Association, on and after January 1, 1867. The embarrassed state of the country, however, supervening upon the close of the war, still continuing, it was not deemed wise to urge the claims of the Association for immediate contributions or subscriptions. The secretary visited local and state conferences and associations, wherever and whenever circumstances would allow, usually receiving an attentive, though very brief hearing, and always cordial indorsements. Through the "Congregational Quarterly," in every issue; through the denominational papers generally, and especially through the "Congregationalist" of this city; through printed circulars, as well as by direct appeals from every pulpit to which he could gain access, and a very large correspondence, —he labored to bring and keep this subject before not an altogether susceptible, nor an altogether willing people. The obstacles which had limited the success of his worthy predecessors, were still multitudinous, but unreasonable; and so, of course, the harder to remove. He gave much time still to the increase of the library, and added, in two years, four thousand six hundred and seventy-nine bound volumes, and over fifteen thousand pamphlets, embracing many of the most rare and valuable works now in the library.

During this time he — with others of this Board — was in earnest pursuit of a suitable site for the proposed House. No person, unfamiliar with this, for so long a time, fruitless search, could conceive the difficulties attending it. The limits within which it must be found, were restricted to Tremont Street on the west, Boylston Street on the south, Washington Street on the east, and School Street on the north, or in the immediate vicinities thereof; and then said site must be large, light, have fair business facilities, yet be reasonably retired. A number of places were found where a part of these necessary conditions were fulfilled, but not all.

The Gardner House, No. 7 Beacon Street, was early looked at, and given up as too small; and at the same time efforts were made to secure estates in its rear, opening into Pemberton Square, but without success. Failing everywhere else, attention was again called to the Gardner House, and a refusal of it taken early in 1871. While casting about to see how necessary accommodations could be crowded into so small a compass, or from what direction any enlargement could be made available, most unexpectedly it was found that the adjoining Club House could be purchased at a fair price, affording ample room, light, air, business facilities, quiet, — indeed, fulfilling all the necessary conditions of the required site; so the purchase of both estates was made at once, for the sum of two hundred and ninety-three thousand four hundred and eighty-four dollars and twelve cents.

But the subject of raising funds to pay for a site and erect a suitable building, was a very frequently recurring subject. At a regular meeting of the directors, Oct. 3, 1869, the question of "What shall be done in the immediate future?" was considered with this one special object in view, but specific action was deferred to secure a full meeting of the Board, which was held Nov. 3, 1869, and a committee was then appointed to devise and put in requisition the best means to secure subscriptions for this purpose.

At a regular meeting held Jan. 5, 1870, the question of the expediency of observing the two hundred and fiftieth anniversary of the landing of the Pilgrims, was presented by the corresponding secretary, and fully discussed. It was answered unanimously in the affirmative, and a committee was appointed to correspond "with other Congregational bodies in regard to the necessary preliminary measures." Cordial responses were generally received, and a convention of delegates from the different parts of the country was held in the chapel of the Broadway Tabernacle Church, of New York city, March 2, 1870, to devise and suggest fitting methods for observing the year, and the subject of erecting the Congregational House, at Boston, was recommended as one of *the three* adopted and indorsed for general memorial gifts. A national convention, held in Chicago the following April, cordially approved of this object, and similar commendations were given at different and nearly all the state associations and conferences during that year. During the last half of this, and all of the following year, the corresponding secretary presented the claims of this object from one to three times on nearly every Sabbath, and in not a few instances received very liberal responses. He spent much time in attendance upon local memorial conventions held in different parts of the State. Deacon Ezra Farnsworth, chairman of the committee on subscriptions, and Hon. E. S. Tobey, president of the Association, and chairman of the board of directors, made especial efforts to secure generous gifts from Boston and its immediate vicinity; giving liberally themselves, they were successful in persuading a number of others to follow their good example. By these united and persistent efforts, and including the amount already raised, as the available funds of the Association, the full sum of one hundred and eighty thousand dollars was realized.

It is proper to state in this connection that it has always been the desire of the directors to obtain *one fairly liberal contribution from every Congregational church in the United States*, and to ask for only one. Life-membership was fixed at the very low price of not less than one dollar, in the hope that the members of the Congregational churches would very generally give that small sum, at least, and so become partners in this family structure. But there has been a strange reluctance to give for this object, scarcely reconcilable with fealty to the great principles they profess to hold dear. At this writing, only just two thirds of the Congregational churches of even Massachusetts, a fraction over one third in Connecticut, just three fifths in Rhode Island, and less than one in eight of the remainder of the Congregational churches in the country, have given anything, either by contributions or personal gifts. Of the two hundred thousand dollars already received and pledged, less than fifty-five thousand has come from outside of Boston and immediate vicinity.

A plan for changing the two buildings, known as the Club and Gardner Houses, so as to make them available for the general purposes of the Association, was presented by Messrs. Cummings and Sears, — well-known architects of this city, — involving an estimated cost of over one hundred and thirty-five thousand dollars. But, at the very best, the probable resources of the directors would not exceed one hundred thousand dollars, and the two mortgages of one hundred thousand dollars each, already on the estates, were an effective protest against further incumbrances ; and yet the two buildings were soon to be without occupants, and so without income ; and something *must be done*. A plan was finally developed in the building committee, and outlined as a guide to the architects for details, for the general arrangements of which they are not to be held responsible, but which was adopted with entire unanimity by the directors, and in nearly every essential feature has been executed by the builders. This plan contemplated in the outset no changes in either of the buildings except where necessity compelled them, and then the least possible; and no changes anywhere that would be likely to be otherwise than permanent, thus preserving floors, partitions, ceilings, cornices, centre-pieces, pilasters, arches, plastering, doors, closets, and the like, greatly economizing the cost of reconstruction, while securing the general convenience of those who were to occupy the different rooms of the building. Upon this plan contracts were made for the chief work needed to be done within the one hundred thousand dollars, hopefully, at the command of the building committee.

As a means chiefly to make sure the needed one hundred thousand dollars, the kind offer, from a number of influential and competent ladies, to get up and conduct a fair in the interests of the building fund, was cordially accepted; and at a meeting of the directors, April 8, 1872, a committee was appointed to arrange for and take the general management of the same. It was held for two weeks in Horticultural Hall, the last of October. It opened with the most encouraging prospects of success; but on the third day the threatened epizoötic was fully developed, cutting off all communication from without, and intercommunications from within the city, so far — and that was very far — as these depended on conveyance by horse-cars or carriages. This embargo continued until near the close of the two weeks, greatly circumscribing our receipts, and disappointing our apparently well-founded hopes. A trifle over fifteen thousand dollars clear gain was realized. The directors wish here to make grateful mention of the earnest and skillful labors and plans of the executive committee, as well as of the officers and attendants at the various tables, and of the churches and individuals who contributed money, time, influence, and variously, to ensure the success that was realized. While all did so much and so well, it may seem invidious to name any one; and yet it is but just to record the fact that Mr. and Mrs. J. C. Clapp took especial interest and rendered especial service from the incipiency to the finale of this toilsome undertaking. To the suggestion that we might be obliged to resort to the expedient of a fair to raise funds, Mrs. Clapp responded heartily more than a year before any decided steps were taken to have one. She conversed with and so interested other ladies that they joined her in the proffer which was so cordially made. She visited cities and towns in its behalf, secured pledges for the refreshment room, and contributed in many ways to the exceedingly pleasant social intercourse of its attendants and visitors, from the beginning to the end.

Owing to the occupancy of the Gardner House, under a lease, the directors were delayed in commencing the work of reconstruction quite beyond their hopes. Plans were accepted at their meeting, held May 4, 1872, and contracts for the heavier part of the work were very soon thereafter made. Verbal assurances were given that all would be complete by the first of November following. Some unlooked-for hinderances intervened, and it was not until the first of February, 1873, that possession was given to any of the occupants. One after another followed, so that before March 1st all the benevolent societies, save one, intending to be here, were in their places. For the names of builders, and the finances of the Association, see pages 46 and 47.

Thus far is history. Without venturing to prophesy, but judging from the unanimous testimony of the constituency of the various Christian organizations now brought together in these exceedingly pleasant rooms, the very confident opinion may be expressed that "the Congregational House" will much more than meet the expectations of its most ardent friends, and will be quite satisfactory to the churches generally, in whose interests it has been erected. When the library building shall be completed, — and may that happy day be near! — the representatives of the principles and polity of the Apostles and Pilgrims will have a home, a centre of influence for good, and a name and a place in Christ's family of churches, as never before.

# ACT OF INCORPORATION

OF THE

# American Congregational Association.

---

## COMMONWEALTH OF MASSACHUSETTS.

*In the Year One Thousand Eight Hundred and Fifty-Four.*

AN ACT to incorporate the Congregational Library Association, at Boston.

*Be it enacted by the Senate and House of Representatives in General Court assembled, and by the authority of the same, as follows:—*

SECTION 1. Rufus Anderson, Joseph S. Clark. Julius A. Palmer, their associates and successors, are hereby made a corporation by the name of the Congregational Library Association at Boston, for the purpose of establishing and perpetuating a library of the religious history and literature of New England, and for the erection of a suitable building for the accommodation of the same, and for the use of charitable societies; with all the powers and privileges, and subject to all the duties, restrictions, and liabilities set forth in the forty-fourth chapter of the Revised Statutes.

SECTION 2. Said corporation may hold real or personal estate, necessary and convenient for the purposes aforesaid, to an amount not exceeding, in the whole, one hundred and fifty thousand dollars, the income whereof shall be devoted to the aforesaid purposes.

[Approved by the Governor, April 12, 1854.

---

## COMMONWEALTH OF MASSACHUSETTS.

*In the Year One Thousand Eight Hundred and Fifty-Six.*

AN ACT to authorize the Congregational Library Association of Boston to hold additional real and personal estate.

*Be it enacted, etc., as follows:—*

SECTION 1. The Congregational Library Association, at Boston, is hereby authorized to hold real and personal estate to the amount of one hundred and fifty thousand dollars, in addition to the amount that said corporation is now authorized by law to hold; provided, that no part of said amount shall be invested in real estate, except in the purchase of a suitable site, and the erection or preparation of a suitable building, to be used for the purposes of said corporation, as set forth in the act of incorporation passed April twelfth, in the year eighteen hundred and fifty-four.

SECTION 2. This act shall take effect from and after its passage.

[Approved by the Governor, April 24, 1856.

## COMMONWEALTH OF MASSACHUSETTS.

*In the Year One Thousand Eight Hundred and Sixty-Four.*

AN ACT concerning the Congregational Library Association.

*Be it enacted, etc., as follows:* —

SECTION 1. The Congregational Library Association is hereby authorized to change its name, and to take the name of the American Congregational Association.

SECTION 2. In addition to the powers heretofore granted said corporation, it is hereby authorized to do such acts as may promote the interest of Congregational churches; by publishing works; by furnishing libraries and pecuniary aid to parishes, churches, and Sabbath Schools; by promoting friendly intercourse and co-operation among Congregational ministers and churches, and with other denominations; and by collecting and disbursing funds for the above objects.

SECTION 3. This act shall take effect on its passage.

[Approved by the Governor, May 10, 1864.

---

## COMMONWEALTH OF MASSACHUSETTS.

*In the Year One Thousand Eight Hundred and Seventy-One.*

AN ACT to authorize the American Congregational Association to hold additional real and personal estate.

*Be it enacted, etc., as follows:* —

SECTION 1. The American Congregational Association, at Boston, is hereby authorized to hold real and personal estate to the amount of four hundred and fifty thousand dollars, in addition to the amount that said corporation is now authorized by law to hold.

SECTION 2. This act shall take effect upon its passage.

[Approved by the Governor, February 24, 1871.

# CONSTITUTION.

ART. I. The name of this body shall be the AMERICAN CONGREGATIONAL ASSOCIATION.

ART. II. The object of this Association shall be to secure the erection, in the city of Boston, of a CONGREGATIONAL HOUSE for the meetings of the body, the accommodation of its library, and for the furtherance of its general purposes; to found and perpetuate a library of books, pamphlets, and manuscripts, and a collection of portraits and relics of the past; and to do whatever else — within the limits of its charter — shall serve to illustrate Congregational history and promote the general interests of the Congregational churches.

ART. III. This Association shall be composed of members of Orthodox Congregational churches, paying each one dollar, or more, into its Treasury.

ART. IV. The officers of this Association shall be a President, such a number of Vice-Presidents as the Association may from year to year elect, a Corresponding and Recording Secretary, a Librarian, Treasurer, Assistant Treasurer, and an Auditor. These Secretaries, Librarian, and Treasurer, with fourteen others, shall be a Board of Directors, charged with the general interests of the Association, five of whom shall constitute a quorum for the transaction of business. These officers shall be chosen by ballot, at the Annual Meetings.

ART. V. The Annual Meetings for the choice of officers, and for other business appropriate to such meetings, shall be held in Boston, on the Tuesday preceding the last Wednesday in May, in each year, at twelve o'clock, M. Special meetings may be called at any time by the Board of Directors. The Annual and all special meetings must be called by published notice in the Orthodox Congregational weekly newspapers of Boston, at least one week previous.

ART. VI. This Constitution may be altered at any Annual Meeting by a vote of two thirds of the members present, public notice having been given of the nature of the proposed alteration in the call for the meeting: but the *third article* shall be unalterable.

# BY-LAWS.

ART. I. The exercises of the Annual Meeting shall be prayer, hearing the report of the Directors, and other officers having reports to make; action upon the same; the election of officers, and the performance of such other business as shall properly come before the meeting.

ART. II. The Directors shall prescribe their own times of meeting, as their judgment of the best interests of the Association may suggest, and the method of calling the same. All their meetings shall be opened with prayer. They shall also have power to appoint and order any public meeting of the Association for anniversary purposes, which they may think fit.

Art. III. At the first Directors' meeting after their appointment, a chairman shall be chosen by ballot, and a Finance Committee and Library Committee by nomination (each of three members), to serve respectively for the year. Immediately after the opening of each meeting the minutes of the previous meeting shall be read, and a docket of business, prepared by the Corresponding Secretary and Librarian, shall be presented to the Board for action, to which any member may add other items.

Art. IV. The Directors shall make a report of their doings for the year at each Annual Meeting of the Association, and suggest such measures for the action of the body as in their judgment its welfare requires.

Art. V. The Corresponding Secretary shall discharge the duties ordinarily belonging to that office.

Art. VI. The Recording Secretary shall make a full record of whatever business is transacted in the meetings, both of the Association and of the Board of Directors, in a book provided for that purpose, and kept at the rooms of the Association.

Art. VII. The Treasurer shall have charge of all moneys belonging to the Association, and hold the same at the disposal of the Directors, who shall also define the duties and responsibilities of the Assistant Treasurer, — paying only such bills as have the certified approval of at least two members of the Finance Committee. He shall report the state of the Treasury to the Association at their Annual Meetings, and to the Directors whenever desired by them to do so.

Art. VIII. The Librarian shall keep a complete catalogue of all books, pamphlets, manuscripts, periodicals, portraits, and other articles of interest belonging to the Association, with the names of their donors annexed, and shall have the general charge of the same under the Library Committee.

Art. IX. Previously to each Annual Meeting, the Library Committee shall examine the Library and all the property of the Association, and report its condition to the Board, who shall embody that statement in their Annual Report.

Art. X. No book, pamphlet, manuscript, or periodical, shall be taken from the Library except on such terms, and for such time, as the Library Committee shall prescribe ; nor shall visitors be permitted to make extracts from manuscripts without the knowledge and consent of the Librarian.

Art. XI. These By-Laws may be amended at any regularly-called meeting of the Association, by a vote of two thirds of the members present.

# OFFICERS

OF THE

# American Congregational Association,

FOR 1872-3.

---

**President.**

HON. EDWARD S. TOBEY, Boston.

**Vice-Presidents.**

Hon. WILLIAM W. THOMAS, Portland, Me.
Rev. NATHANIEL BOUTON, D. D., Concord, N. H.
Rev. HARVEY D. KITCHEL, D. D., Middlebury, Vt.
Rev. JACOB IDE, D. D., Medway, Mass.
Rev. SETH SWEETSER, D. D., Worcester, Mass.
Hon. SAMUEL WILLISTON, Easthampton, Mass.
Rev. THOMAS SHEPARD, D. D., Bristol, R. I.
Hon. AMOS C. BARSTOW, Providence, R. I.
Rev. LEONARD BACON, D. D., New Haven, Conn.
Hon. WILLIAM A. BUCKINGHAM, Norwich, Conn.
Hon. CALVIN DAY, Hartford, Conn.
Rev. WILLIAM M. TAYLOR, D. D., New York City.
Rev. RAY PALMER, D. D., New York City.
Rev. WM. IVES BUDINGTON, D. D., Brooklyn, N. Y.
Rev. ISRAEL W. ANDREWS, D. D., Marietta, O.
Rev. SAMUEL WOLCOTT, D. D., Cleveland, O.
Rev. NATHANIEL A. HYDE, Indianapolis, Ind.
Rev. JULIAN M. STURTEVANT, D. D., Jacksonville, Ill.
Rev. SAMUEL C. BARTLETT, D. D., Chicago, Ill.
Hon. CHARLES G. HAMMOND, Chicago, Ill.
A. FINCH, Esq., Milwaukee, Wis.
Rev. WM. E. MERRIMAN, D. D., Ripon, Wis.
Rev. TRUMAN M. POST, D. D., St. Louis, Mo.
Rev. WILLIAM SALTER, D. D., Burlington, Iowa.
Rev. GEORGE MOOAR, D. D., Oakland, Cal.
Rev. HENRY WILKES, D. D., Montreal, Canada.

**Directors.**

Hon. EDWARD S. TOBEY, Boston.
JOHN FIELD, Esq., Arlington.
Rev. ALONZO H. QUINT, D. D., New Bedford.
EZRA FARNSWORTH, Esq., Boston.
Rev. H. M. DEXTER, D. D., Boston.
HENRY D. HYDE, Esq., Boston.
Rev. JOHN O. MEANS, D. D., Boston.
JAMES P. MELLEDGE, Esq., Cambridge.
Hon. RUFUS S. FROST, Chelsea.
J. RUSSELL BRADFORD, Esq., Boston.
WM. C. STRONG, Esq., Brighton.
DAVID N. SKILLINGS, Esq., Winchester.
Rev. N. G. CLARK, D. D., Boston.
RICHARD H. STEARNS, Esq., Boston.

**Treasurer.**

SAMUEL T. SNOW, ESQ., Boston

**Corresponding Secretary, Librarian, and Assistant Treasurer.**

REV. ISAAC P. LANGWORTHY, Chelsea.

**Recording Secretary.**

REV. DANIEL P. NOYES, Longwood.

**Auditor.**

JOSEPH N. BACON, ESQ., Newton.

www.ingramcontent.com/pod-product-compliance
Lightning Source LLC
LaVergne TN
LVHW011119110826
845150LV00008B/2181